The Developers' Dictionary
and Handbook

The Developers' Dictionary and Handbook

Koder M. Collison

Lexington Books
D.C. Heath and Company
Lexington, Massachusetts
Toronto   London

Library of Congress Cataloging in Publication Data

Collison, Koder M
The developers' dictionary and handbook.

1. Industrial sites—United States—Dictionaries. 2. Industrial promotion—United States—Dictionaries. I. Title.
HD1393.5.C64   338'.0025'73   73-21866
ISBN 0-669-92882-8

Sponsored in part by a grant from the A.I.D.C. Educational Foundation.

Copyright © 1974 by D.C. Heath and Company

Published simultaneously in Canada.

Printed in the United States of America.

International Standard Book Number: 0-669-92882-8

Library of Congress Catalog Card Number: 73-21866

To SIBYL . . .

A lady of few words at a time when silence was indeed golden . . . without whose patience and forbearance this compilation could not have been completed.

Table of Contents

Foreword

At last we have a dictionary and handbook that provides us with ready reference to terms and material used in our practice of industrial development. The need has been recognized for a number of years, but no one ever "got around" to doing the job.

We of the industrial development fraternity are, therefore, beholden to Koder M. Collison for his enterprise, dedication, and courage. Yes —courage, for as Dr. Samuel Johnson observed:

No dictionary of a living tongue ever can be perfect since—while it is hastening to publication—some words are budding and some are falling away.

It follows that considerable fortitude is required of the author, for there is the inevitability of carping criticism from persons who do not agree with the material offered.

A ready reference work designed for a special field of endeavor requires that the reader have faith in the author's qualifications. One may indeed have full confidence in Koder Collison. He is a Fellow of the American Industrial Development Council, a Certified Industrial Developer and a professional with over thirty years of active practice in industrial development. His experience ranges from local municipal development work to a position as development director of one of the nation's largest railroad networks. Mr. Collison has headed the development departments for two states, having served in cabinet-level positions with three governors. Prior to his well-earned retirement early in 1974, he was Director of Industrial Development for the Appalachian Regional Commission, a states-federal agency designed to improve the economy of a thirteen-state area extending from southern New York State to the northeastern portion of Mississippi.

Mr. Collison's "Developer's Dictionary and Handbook" is the result of a compilation of terms over a period of some ten years. It is indeed a valuable addition to the library of authoritative material on *industrial development; that process which enhances the socioeconomic environment of an area through the creation and the preservation of productive employment opportunities.*

On behalf of all those engaged in this vital field, we compliment Mr. Collison and express our gratitude to him for this contribution to our practice.

Richard Preston, HLM-FM/AIDC, CID
President
American Industrial Development Council
Wenham, Mass.   Educational Foundation

ix

Preface

The scholarly lexicographer will find that this volume is not truly a dictionary. Certainly, the purist will complain that the form of this book lacks those elements most often found in such. There is no attempt to syllabicate the definitions herein, nor are pronunciations set forth. It is the intent, rather, to present the meanings of common, and some uncommon, terms used with some frequency in the world of the developer, whether he be in real estate, area development, architecture, engineering, or the many other disciplines concerned with economic development.

Over the years, a number of glossaries have been published by various organizations and individuals in the general field of area development. Most of these have been appended as an after thought to books covering the general practice of economic development. However, there has been no comprehensive compendium of terms and definitions available for general usage.

This book, then, is designed to assemble in one volume the words, terms, and phrases which may prove most helpful to those in the fields of economic development, whether they be expert or newcomer to the business.

More than 2,900 terms are included in the definitions section. They cover a wide spectrum of many disciplines including, among others: agronomy, architecture, accounting, construction, engineering, law, transportation, and utilities.

Some of the definitions may seem strange. For example, a *fairway* is not defined as a piece of a golf course. Nor is a *boss* a supervisor. And a *groin* probably is not your immediate interpretation. Actually, the definitions set forth herein are directed toward translating the usage of words and phrases in the context of the developer, architect, realtor, and others engaged in furthering, or at least promoting, the economy of an area.

It will be noted that considerable space is given to some definitions while other terms are defined in a word or two. New definitions are presented for *new plant, new operation, expansion,* etc. Hopefully, this may be helpful in arriving at standardization of reporting industrial activities in communities and regions.

The "Handbook" section includes tables, sample forms, and supporting material further defining the work of the developer. Here again, no effort has been made to include every conceivable table or reference, instead, I have tried to present those bits of information which should prove most helpful to developers.

In effect, this is not a textbook, per se, but rather a reference volume to be used in conjunction with textbooks such as Bessire's *The Practice of*

Industrial Development or Kinnard's *Industrial Real Estate,* the latter sponsored by the Society of Industrial Realtors.

The suggestions and comments of users of this publication will be greatly appreciated by the compiler.

Koder M. Collison

Acknowledgments

Many organizations and individuals were more than helpful in the compilation of the *Developer's Dictionary and Handbook*. Among those to whom I owe a special thanks for their efforts in assisting me are the following:

Frederick J.A. Beyer, Indianapolis Chamber of Commerce, Indianapolis, Indiana

Vincent J. Floyd, Assistant Vice President of The Penn Central Transportation Company, and members of his staff, including: V.L. Candy, E.C. Christ, F.W. Fredericks, R.L. Hayes, Evelyn H. Mills, O.R. Pendy, and G. Shimrak

Professor Howard G. Roepke, CID, Department of Geography, University of Illinois, Urbana

Salim Kublawi, Economist, Appalachian Regional Commission, Washington, D.C.

Joseph Matyi, Esq., Appalachian Regional Commission, Washington, D.C.

Everett S. Preston, President, E.S. Preston & Associates, Inc., Columbus, Ohio

Robert Rine, Director Area Development, American Electric Power Company, New York, New York

Robert Wolf, Director Area Development, Ohio Power Company, Canton, Ohio

. . . And, of course, Richard Preston, president of the AIDC Educational Foundation, without whose encouragement this publication would not have seen the light of day.

The Dictionary

A

ABANDONMENT. The discontinuance of all or part of a line of a railroad or the operation thereof by a carrier; also the proceeding whereby authority for such discontinuance is sought.

ABATEMENT. Amount deducted from a bill or debt for any cause.

ABATTOIR. A place where livestock is slaughtered.

ABEYANCE. Suspension; postponement.

ABROGATE. Annul; abolish; cancel; abandon.

ABSOLUTE ZERO. Hypothetical temperature at which a substance is totally deprived of heat: $-459.7°$ Fahrenheit.

ABSORPTION OF SWITCHING. Railroad carriers, in certain instances, "absorb" switching charges made by another delivering railroad to consignee, thus relieving both shipper and receiver of these costs.

ABSTRACT OF TITLE. A document containing a brief statement of the original grant and subsequent conveyances and encumbrances with respect to transfer of title of real estate.

ABUTMENT. (1) A supporting or buttressing structure, as at the end of a bridge. (2) That part of an arch that bears the main thrust or strain of a structure.

AB VOLT. One-hundred-millionth of a volt.

AB WATT. One-thousandth of a watt.

AC, ALTERNATING CURRENT. An electric current that reverses its direction regularly and continuously.

ACCELERATED AMORTIZATION. A procedure of amortizing for tax purposes over a five-year period the depreciable property cost of plant and equipment; authorized by the U.S. government in the interest of defense production. Also, some facilites designed for air and/or water pollution control are accorded *accelerated amortization* by some state and federal taxing agencies.

ACCELERATOR. A mixture added to concrete mix for rapid hardening of the cement.

ACCEPTANCE. (1) Agreement by a receiver of negotiable paper to pay the value of same. (2) Agreement to terms offered.

ACCESS. The legal right to cross another's property in order to reach one's own land.

ACCESSORIAL SERVICE. A service rendered by a carrier in addition to transportation (e.g., temporary storage of goods, etc.)

ACCESS ROAD. A road giving access to a property and connecting with an "open route" or main highway.

ACCLIVITY. An upward slope.

ACCOMMODATION LADDER. A stairway or ladder hung over the side of a seagoing vessel.

1

ACCOMMODATION TRAIN. A local passenger train stopping at all stations between main terminals; a commuter or commutation train.

ACCOUNT. Statement of sums and amounts due from one person to another and their offsets arising from mutual transactions; a summary of debits and credits.

ACCOUNTS PAYABLE. Current expense debts.

ACCOUNTS RECEIVABLE. Current debts owed to a company; credits.

ACCOUTERMENTS, ACCOUTREMENTS. Equipment; trappings.

ACCRETION. The increase or extension of the boundaries of land by action of natural forces such as shoreline erosion by water.

ACCRUAL BASIS. An account kept in such a manner as to show earned income and expense without regard to actual received income and disbursements.

ACCRUE. (1) To increase. (2) To accumulate, as interest or dividends.

ACCUMULATED PROVISION. (1) Reserve. (2) Depletion allowance.

ACIERATE. To convert to steel.

ACKNOWLEDGMENT. A receipt.

A COMPTE (French). On account; part payment.

ACOUSTICAL TILE. A material designed to absorb and thus deaden sound in a room or building. Usually installed in ceilings and walls.

ACQUEST. Something acquired by means other than inheritance.

ACQUITTANCE. (1) A written receipt of full payment. (2) Discharge from all claims.

ACRE. 43,560 square feet; approximately 208.7 feet squared; 160 square rods; 4,840 square yards. (Legend has it that an acre is equivalent to the area a yoke of oxen can plow in a day.)

ACREAGE. Acres collectively; the number of acres in a tract of land. (See "Estimating Acreage"—Handbook section.)

ACRE FOOT. The quantity of water that would cover one acre to a depth of one foot; 43,560 cubic feet.

ACRE INCH. 3,360 cubic feet.

ACTA. Minutes of a court proceeding.

ACT OF GOD. A happening for which no one is personally liable, as an accident due to natural causes such as a flood, etc.

ACTUARIALLY SOUND. The determination that an investment will pay out; that a property will continue its usefulness through the amortization period.

ACTUARY. A person whose work it is to calculate risks, etc.

ADDENDUM. A supplement or appendix; a thing added or to be added.

AD HOC COMMITTEE. A committee appointed or formed for a specific purpose.

ADIABATIC. Of or denoting change in volume or pressure without loss or gain in heat.

AD INFINITUM. Without limit.

ADIT. A mine entrance.

ADJACENT. Adjoining or abutting.

ADJUDICATE. (1) To hear and decide a legal case. (2) To determine judicially.

ADJURATION. An earnest entreaty; a plea.

ADJUSTMENT. Settlement or compromise of the amount to be paid in case of loss or claim.

AD LIBITUM. Ad lib; to speak "off the cuff."

ADMEASURE. Apportion.

ADMINISTRATOR. (1) A person appointed by a court to settle the estate of a person who died without a will. (2) The chief officer of an administrative agency of a government or civic body.

ADORNMENT. A decorative treatment or ornamental object on the side of a building.

ADSCRIPT. A postscript; something written after.

ADUNC. Curving inward.

AD VALOREM. (1) In proportion to value. (2) *Ad valorem taxes* usually refers to real property taxes.

ADVERSE HYDRO. Adverse water conditions limiting the production of hydroelectric power.

ADVERSE POSSESSION. The right of an occupant of land to acquire title against the real owner when possession has been actual, visible, and continuous for a statutory period.

ADVOCATE. A person who pleads another's cause.

ADVOCATUS DIABOLI. (1) Devil's advocate; one who espouses an argument in which he doesn't necessarily agree but does so in order to stimulate replies to such stand.

AEGIS, EGIS. (1) Sponsorship. (2) Protective power.

AEROMETER. A device for measuring the weight and density of air.

AERUGO. Copper rust.

AESTHETICS. Study or theory of beauty.

AFFIANT. One who makes an affidavit.

AFFIDAVIT. An instrument containing a sworn statement.

AFFILIATE. A company associated with another but not necessarily a subsidiary.

AFFOREST. To convert land into woodlands.

AFFRANCHISE. To free or liberate from bondage or obligation.

AFTERBURNER. A device for injecting fuel into the exhaust system of a jet engine to increase its thrust.

AFTERDAMP. A mixture of gases resulting from mine fire or explosion and most dangerous to breathe.

AGENDA. The program prepared for formal meetings setting forth the priority of items to be considered for discussion.

AGENT. (1) Representative. (2) An *industrial agent* represents the interests of his organization in inducing industries to locate or expand in his area and in assisting in the preparation of the area for economic growth. (3) A *real estate agent* may represent an organization (such as a utility) in the sale of property owned by that company or he may represent the company which is in search of a plant site.

AGGLOMERATE. A cluster; mass.

AGGRADATION. The build-up of a grade or slope by sediment deposition, as in the bank of a stream.

AGGREGATES. Mineral fragments used as ballast on railroads and as a mixture for roadbuilding.

AGIO. The fee paid to exchange one kind of money for another.

AGIOTAGE. Stock speculation.

AGITATOR BODY. A truck body designed for mixing concrete enroute to a building site.

AGNATE. Related on the male side of the family.

AGONIC LINE. Line on which the direction of the magnetic needle is true north.

AGRARIAN. (1) Pertaining to land or farming. (2) One who farms. (3) One who espouses more equitable distribution of land.

AGREEMENT. A contract.

AGREEMENT OF SALE. A purchase agreement between buyer and seller.

AGRÉMENS. Amenities; embellishments.

AGRONOMY. (1) Field crop production and soil management. (2) The application of scientific principles to farming.

AIR MILE. One-sixtieth of a degree of the earth's equator: 6,080.2 feet.

ALCALDE. A mayor of a Spanish-American town or pueblo.

ALCAN HIGHWAY. The highway from British Columbia to Fairbanks, Alaska—1,527 miles.

ALDERMAN. Council member of a city government who ranks below the mayor or principal officer.

ALGA, ALGAE, ALGI, Plants containing chlorophyl but having no real root leaf or stem. (Found in still water.)

ALIDADE. A surveying instrument used in topographic mapping.

ALIENEE. One who takes over transferred property.

ALIENOR. A vendor of property; a seller.

ALIUNIDE. Evidence from a source other than that directly concerned with the case at hand.

ALKALI. Any base, such as soda, that is soluble in water and can neutralize acids.

ALKYD. Resin used in paints.

ALLOCATUR. The judicial endorsement of a writ.

ALLOW. (1) To yield to another's gain. (2) To concede. (3) To discount.

ALLOY STEEL. Steel containing more than 1.65 percent manganese or more than 0.60 percent of other elements added for the purpose of modifying the mechanical or physical properties normally possessed by carbon steel.

ALLUVIAL. Pertaining to or composed of earth deposited by water.

ALTERNATING CURRENT(AC). An electric current that reverses its direction regularly and continuously.

ALTERNATOR. A device which produces alternating current.

ALUMINA. An oxide of aluminum found in bauxite.

ALUMINUM. Metal produced by reducing alumina by electric power.

AMBIANCE, AMBIENCE. Environment; surrounding milieu.

AMBIENT AIR. Refers to the surrounding atmosphere; all space outside buildings, stacks, or exterior ducts. (Air purity standards for a specific area are often referred to as "ambient air quality standards.")

AMENITIES. (1) Attractive, desirable features. (2) Cultural, recreational, spiritual, civic, and educational facilities.

AMERICAN PLAN. All-inclusive charge made by a hotel which includes room, board, and certain services.

AMICUS CURIAE. Friend of the court; a person called in to advise the court on some legal matter.

AMORAL. Not concerned with ethical or moral distinctions or judgments.

AMORTIZATION. (1) The liquidation of a financial obligation on an installment basis. (2) The process of gradually extinguishing debt by a series of periodic payments to a creditor.

AMPERE. (1) The flow of electrons in an electric current. (2) A unit of electric current proportional to the quantities of electrons through a conductor past a given point in one second. (3) The unit current produced in a circuit by one volt acting through a resistance of one ohm.

ANABATIC. Upward rising air currents.

ANACLINAL. Lying across the dip of the rocks; having a course opposed to the dip of the underlying rocks.

ANACOUSTIC. Without sound.

ANALOGOUS. Resembling; similar to.

ANCILLARY. Auxiliary; subsidiary.

ANELE. Annoint; oil.

ANHYDRATE. To dry; dehydrate.

ANHYDROUS. Destitute of water.

ANIMAL HUSBANDRY. The breeding and raising of farm animals.

ANION. A negative ion.

ANNAL. The record of a single year.

ANNALS. A record of events year by year.

ANNEAL. To strengthen and temper by heating and cooling slowly to prevent brittleness of the material.

ANNEX. A building addition or a building auxiliary to the purposes of the main building.

ANNEXATION. The addition of territory to a governmental entity, such as bringing in a portion of a county within a city limits.

ANNUITY. (1) Yearly payment. (2) An investment yielding fixed payments.

ANODE. The positive electrode toward which anions migrate in any electrolytic cell.

ANODIZE. To put a protective oxide film on a metal by means of electrolysis.

ANTHRACITE. (1) Hard coal. (2) Almost a pure carbon coal that burns slowly, with little flame, but emitting high heat.

ANTICATALYST. A substance that retards chemical reaction.

ANTICLINAL. Inclined in opposite directions.

ANTICLINORIUM. A system of parallel folds in stratified rock having a rolling topography.

ANTIMONY. A silver-white, hard metallic element often used in metal alloys.

ANTITRUST. Opposed to trusts, cartels, pools, monopolies, etc.

APOGEE. Highest point.

APOLITICAL. Not concerned with politics or the political world.

APPELANT. An appeal or one who a makes the appeal.

APPOSITE. Relevant.

APPRAISAL. An estimate of quality, quantity, or value.

APPRAISAL BY CAPITALIZATION. An estimate of value by capitalization of productivity and income.

APPRAISAL BY COMPARISON. Comparability of value to sales price of nearby or similar properties.

APPRAISAL BY SUMMATION. Adding together parts of property separately appraised to form the whole.

APPRAISER. One who is given the authority to estimate the value of property.

APPRECIATE. Rise in value.

APPRISE. To inform.

APPRIZE. To appraise.

APPURTENANCES. (1) Incidental rights and interests that attach to and pass with the transfer of land. (2) Adjuncts; accessory items.

APRON. (1) A bridge structure supporting railroad tracks connecting the car deck of a car ferry with the tracks extending to the land, hinged on the shore so that it may be moved vertically at the outboard end to accommodate varying elevations of the tide. (2) A paved area at an airport designed for the parking and tying down planes for temporary storage.

APRON TRACK. Railroad track along the waterfront edge of a pier or wharf for direct transfer of cargo between ship and railroad car.

APSE. The projecting part of a building (especially of a church), usually semicircular with vaulted ceiling.

AQUA REGIA. An acid mixture capable of dissolving gold and platinum.

AQUIFER. A strata capable of conveying or supplying water.

ARBITER. Umpire; referee; mediator.

ARBITRATION. Settlement of a dispute by a person chosen to hear both sides of an argument and arrive at a decision.

ARCADE. A passageway having an arched roof.

ARCHITECT. A designer of buildings, etc., who generally supervises the construction in order that plans are carried out as scheduled.

ARCHITRAVE. The part of an entablature that rests upon the column heads and supports a frieze.

AREA. (1) Length × width. (2) Square footage; acreage, etc.

ARÈTE. A mountain ridge.

ARGIL. White clay used in pottery products.

ARGILLACEOUS LIMESTONE. Clay-like limestone.

ARPENT (FRENCH). About an acre of land.

ARREARAGE. (1) An obligation not met on time. (2) A thing kept in reserve.

ARRIVAL NOTICE. A notice furnished to a consignee advising of the arrival of freight.

ARROGATE. To claim or seize without right.

ARROYO. A deep gully formed by an intermittent stream.

ARTERIAL HIGHWAY. A main highway designed for through traffic.

ARTESIAN WELL. (1) A free-flowing well or spring. (2) A well penetrating into a water-bearing stratum between impermeable strata from a surface lower than the source of the water out at the surface.

ARTICLES OF PARTNERSHIP. The contract between two or more parties.

ARTISAN. (1) Producer. (2) Fabricator.

ARTISTE. Designer of products.

ASSESSED VALUATION. Valuation of property for tax purposes.

ASSESSMENT. A charge against real estate to cover proportionate cost of an improvement such as a sewer, water line, or paving of a street. Also the assessment made against real estate for property taxes.

ASSETS. Anything owned which has value.

ASSIGN. To transfer in writing the ownership of property.

ASSIGNED CAR. A railroad car assigned to a particular industry or for hauling a specific commodity.

ASSIGNEE. A person to whom an assignment is made (as a trustee for the creditors of a bankrupt estate).

ASSIGNMENT. Transfer of claim (property) from one party to another.

ASSIGNOR. One who transfers his property to assignees for the benefit of creditors or for other reasons.

ASSUMPSIT. (1) An agreement, written, spoken, or implied, but not under seal. (2) Action to recover damages for nonfulfillment of such agreement.

ATELIER. A studio or workshop.

ATRIUM. A hall or entrance court.

ATTACHMENT. Seizure of property by legal procedure.

ATTAINDER. The loss of all civil rights consequent to a sentence of outlawry for a capital offense.

ATTORNEY GENERAL. The chief law officer of a State.

AUCTION. Public sale to the highest bidder.

AUCTIONEER. A person licensed to sell by auction.

AUTARCHY. (1) Absolute rule or sovereignty. (2) Autocracy.

AUTARKY. The policy of establishing independence of imports; to become economically self-sustaining as a nation.

AUTHORIZED CAPITAL. The aggregate of stated value of the shares of stock that a corporation is empowered to use.

AUTONOMOUS. Self-governing; independent.

AVERAGE. (1) The mean value. (2) Medium quality. (3) Fair sample.

AVERAGE AGREEMENT. An agreement made between an industry and a railroad whereby the industry is debited for the time cars are held for loading and unloading beyond a certain agreed period, and credited for the time cars are released within a certain agreed period. Demurrage charges are assessed at the end of the month for any outstanding debits.

AVERAGE ANNUAL DAILY TRAFFIC (AADT). The total yearly highway traffic divided by the number of days in the year.

AVULSION. Removal of land from one owner to another by a stream changing its channel.

AXIOM. A self-evident or universally established or accepted principle or rule.

B

BABBIT METAL. A soft, white alloy of tin, copper, and antimony used as a liner, bushing, or facing.

BACK HAUL. (1) In the event a railroad carrier has transported a shipment beyond its intended destination, the carrier is required to *back haul* the shipment to the proper destination as indicated on the bill of lading for that particular shipment. (2) Traffic moving in the direction of light flow when a carrier's traffic on a route is heavier in one direction than another.

BACTERIA. Unicellular microorganisms exhibiting both plant and animal characteristics, which may be harmless, helpful or lethal.

BAD ORDER TRACK. A track on which railroad oars in need of repairs are placed.

BAFFLE. A partition or grating in a pipe, tank, or channel to control eddies of liquids and secure a uniform flow.

BAGASSE. The dry refuse of sugar cane after the juice has been removed; used in making fibreboard and some types of paper.

BAIL. (1) An arch-shaped support for a canopy. (2) To deliver; as goods to another's disposition or care without transference of ownership.

BAILIFF. One who oversees an estate for an owner; a steward

BAILMENT. The act of bailing an accused person; goods, etc.

BALANCE. The difference required to make assets and liabilities of a deal balance or become equal.

BALANCE OF TRADE. The ratio of imports and exports between nations or states.

BALLAST. Selected material placed in a railroad road bed for maintaining surface and alignment of tracks.

BALLOON LEASE. A lease under which a tenant agrees to higher rental following an agreed period, usually contingent upon higher maintenance or utility costs to the lessor.

BALUSTER. One of a set of small pillars supporting a handrail.

BALUSTRADE. A handrail supported by a baluster.

BANQUETTE. (1) An extra embankment (or shoulder) to provide a break in surface drainage. (2) A sidewalk.

BAROMETER. An instrument for registering atmospheric pressure, used in forecasting weather and measuring elevations.

BARTER. The practice of trading without the use of cash.

BASE LOAD. The minimum load (electric power).

BASE PRESSURE. Pressure of gas in excess of atmospheric pressure.

BASING POINT SYSTEM. A method of computing delivered prices of certain products; the producer adds to the price set for his product the cost of transportation to a consignee at a published *basing point* without regard to the point of manufacture.

BAS RELIEF. A kind of sculpture in which figures project only slightly from the background, as from a building wall.

BATTEN. (1) A light strip of wood for covering a joint between boards. (2) A strip of sawed timber used for flooring, etc.

BATTLEMENT. A parapet "toothed" along its upper line.

BAUXITE. The principal ore from which aluminum is made.

BAY. The principal open space or division of a structure between columns, walls, or piers.

BAYOU. A marshy inlet (or outlet) of a stream, lake, etc.

BEAM. A horizontal piece forming part of the frame of a building, usually furnlshing support to a roof, floor, or ceiling.

BEARER. One who holds and presents for payment, a note, bill, bank check, or draft.

BED ROCK. The solid rock underlying the superficial formations of the earth's surface.

BEL. A unit expressing the ratio of the values of two amounts of power being the logarithms to the base 10 of their ratios—a measure of sound intensity. (See Handbook section for sundry sound sources and ratings.)

BELL METAL. An alloy of copper and tin used in making bells.

BEMA. A platform, usually part of the church altar.

BENCH. (1) Level elevated ground along a shoreline or slope. (Highway contractors and road builders often create such *benches* in deep cuts to minimize rockfall and landslide dangers.) (2) Shelves and/or ledges created in mining to prevent rockfall.

BENCH MARK. A mark indicating position and elevation used as a reference point in surveys of areas.

BENCH WALL. The abutment or side wall of a culvert or tunnel.

BENT. The group of members forming a single vertical support of a trestle.

BESSEMER CONVERTER. A tilting receptacle lined with acid or a basic material in which molten pig iron is converted to steel.

BESSEMER PROCESS. The conversion of liquid pig iron to steel by forcing air at atmospheric temperature through the metallic bath in a converter in which no extraneous fuel is burned, resulting in the oxidation or reduction of the carbon manganese and silicas to the extent desired and their removal in the form of slag.

BETHEL PROCESS. A full-cell pressure treatment of wood with an oil preservative.

BETON. A concrete made of gravel, sand, cement, and lime.

BEVEL GEAR. A gear having beveled teeth for transmitting rotary motion at an angle.

BEZEL. The bevel on the edge of a cutting tool such as a chisel.

BIANNUAL. Semiannual; twice a year.

BIENNIAL. (1) Every two years. (Occurring every other year.) (2) Lasting for two years.

BIGHT. (1) A bend or curve in a shoreline or stream. (2) The loop of a rope.

BILATERAL. (1) Mutually binding on both of two parties. (2) A figure having two sides.

BILGE. The rounded part of a ship's bottom.

BILLABONG. A stagnant backwater or blind branch of a river.

BILLET. A semi-finished product of a blooming mill, rectangular or square, and having a maximum crosssectional area of 36 square inches and a minimum crosssectional dimension of 9½ square inches.

BILLET CAR. A low-sided railroad car or gondola built entirely of steel for transporting hot billets.

BILL OF EXCHANGE. A written order for the payment of a given sum to a designated person.

BILL OF LADING. A contract for transportation services authorized by tariff.

BILL OF SALE. An instrument attesting to the transfer of property.

BIMONTHLY. An ambiguous term denoting either twice a month or once every two months. Confusion may be avoided by using the term "semimonthly" when appropriate to designate twice a month.

BINDER. A written instrument binding all parties to an agreement.

BINDERY. A place where books are bound and sometimes printed.

BIOCHEMICAL OXYGEN DEMAND (BOD). The amount of oxygen required for bacteria to consume organic water waste.

BIQUARTERLY. Occurring twice each quarter.

BIRTHRIGHT. (1) Heritage. (2) Any right acquired by birth.

BISECT. To divide into two equal parts.

BITT. A post or vertical tier in a ship's deck.

BITUMENS. A mixture of hydrocarbons which are soluble in carbon disulfide.

BITUMINOUS COAL. Soft coal, low in carbon content, which burns with a yellow, smoky flame.

BIWEEKLY. An ambiguous term denoting either twice weekly or once every two weeks. To avoid confusion it is suggested that "semiweekly" be used to designate twice a week.

BLANK ENDORSEMENT. An endorsement on a negotiable instrument that names no payee, therefore making it payable to any bearer.

BLANKET BOND. A bond covering a group of persons, articles, or properties. (A *bonded roof,* for example, is one which is guaranteed for a period of time specified in a *bond* given to the building owner by a roofing contractor.)

BLANKET MORTGAGE. A single mortgage covering more than one piece of real estate. (Note: The mortgagee cannot be required to release any part of the property from his "blanket" until payment is made in full for all of the secured properties.)

BLAST FURNACE. A furnace in which combustion is forced by a current of air under pressure.

BLENDE. One of a number of minerals combining sulfur with a metallic element, such as *pitchblende*.

BLOC. A group or faction.

BLOCK. (1) A section of a railroad of defined limits. (2) A group of railroad cars classified for movement to the same yard or terminal. (3) A pulley, or set of pulleys, in a frame; a *block* and tackle. (4) A "square" of a city bounded by four streets. (5) An office building or group of buildings named for the owner, builder, or other.

BLOCK TIN. Pure tin as distinguished from tin plate.

BLOOM. (1) An earthy mineral found as a powder incrustation on certain ores. (2) A mass of malleable iron. (3) A bar of iron or steel hammered or rolled from an ingot.

BLOOMERY. A forge or furnace for making malleable iron direct from ore.

BLOWDOWN. (1) The act of letting water out of a boiler under pressure for the purpose of reducing the concentration of dissolved or suspended solids. (2) Damage to crops by heavy winds.

BLUE LABEL. Shipment of atomic material by carrier.

BLUNGE. In the ceramic industry, the mixing of clay and water in a pug.

BOARD FOOT. A unit of lumber measuring one foot long, one foot wide, and one inch thick (144 cubic inches).

BOARD OF TRADE. An association such as a Chamber of Commerce, whose dues-paying members usually represent the interests of commerce and industry.

BOAT TRAIN. (1) A train scheduled to connect with a boat. (2) A ship train.

BONA FIDE. Authentic, literally meaning "good faith."

BOND. (1) A binding covenant or agreement. (2) A promise to pay; a note (see "Bond Ratings"—Handbook section).

BONDED CARRIER. An airline, trucking, or railroad company which has deposited a surety with the U.S. Bureau of Customs evidencing its ability to pay the duty on any imported goods transported by the carrier. The use of *bonded carriers* makes possible the development of inland ports, since without bonded transportation, all goods would have to be cleared at border points.

BONDED WAREHOUSE. Operates similarly to a bonded carrier. The owner of the facility acquires a bond which guarantees payment of the duty on all goods stored in the warehouse, and agrees to take precautionary security measures to prevent removal of goods from the warehouse without the express approval of the local customs inspector. No duty need be paid on goods stored in a bonded warehouse until they are removed *in the presence* of a customs inspector. The warehouse may be operated by the individual or company doing the importing, or it may be operated by an independent party.

BONDS (MORTGAGE). Certificates of indebtedness representing long-term borrowing of capital funds.

BONE MEAL. Crushed bones used as fertilizer.

BONUS. A premium paid for obtaining a loan, charter, etc.; a "finder's fee."

BOOK AMOUNTS. The amounts recorded on a company's accounting records at any given time. These may reflect historical cost, original cost, or current value.

BOOK COST. The amount at which assets are recorded in the accounts without deduction of related accumulated provisions for depreciation, amortization, etc.

BOOM. (1) A long pole or spar to extend the bottom of a sail. (2) A long spar or beam projecting from the mast of a derrick to support or guide the object to be lifted or lowered.

BOOMERS. Binder devices for the purpose of tightening chains or steel tapes around cargo on flat cars or flatbed trucks.

BOONDOCKS. Slang expression for hinterlands, outcountry, backwoods areas, and the like.

BORING. (1) A hole made by an auger or drill. (2) A sample of soil or other underlying material, as in a *test boring*.

BOROUGH. An unincorporated town or village (common in Pennsylvania).

BORROW. Material taken from one location to be used for fill at another area.

BORROW PIT. An excavation resulting from obtaining full material.

BOSKET. A thicket or clump of bushes or scrub trees.

BOSS. A projecting ornament on a building or archway.

BOTTOM LAND. (1) Lowland along a river. (2) Very rich soil found in flood plain areas.

BOTTOMRY. A maritime contract pledging a vessel as security for a loan.

BOULE. A small mass of fused alumina tinted to resemble gem stones.

BOUNDS (BOUNDARIES). (In metes and *bounds,* the bounds are artificial and usually natural boundaries such as roads, streams, adjoining property lines and the like which have not been defined by actual survey.)

BOURG, BURG. A village or town.

BOURN. A brook or small stream.

BOURSE. A stock exchange or money market.

BOUSE. To lift or haul with block and tackle.

BOXCAR. A roofed freight car fully enclosed to protect lading from weather and to maintain security of contents. The car usually has sliding doors to facilitate loading and unloading, which may be secured for shipment enroute.

BOYCOTT. A refusal to use or buy a particular product or the products of a particular producer.

BRACKISH. (1) Salty; briny. (2) Distasteful.

BRAD. A small, slender nail.

BRADAWL. A short, sharp-pointed instrument for making shallow holes in wood or other material for *brads* or screws.

BRADLEY WASHER. A community sanitary washing device for use of factory workers.

BRAIN BANK. A consortium of individuals versed in various disciplines whose assistance and expertise may be called upon when required for solving specific problems.

BRANCH LINE. A secondary line of a railroad.

BRANCH PLANT. Any operational facility located in an area other than that occupied by the home or headquarters plant of the company. The branch operation may be larger or smaller than the home plant and may or may not produce similar products.

BREAKWATER. A structure to afford shelter from surf or water wave erosive action.

BRIDGE. Any structure spanning a stream, ravine' roadway, etc.
  (1) *bascule bridge.* A mechanical apparatus of which each end counterbalances the other—a kind of drawbridge.
  (2) *cantilever.* A long structural member lying across a support arch, the projecting arms in balance.
  (3) *drawbridge.* A bridge of which the whole or part may be raised.
  (4) *lift bridge.* A bridge which is lifted upward to allow the passage of vessels.
  (5) *pontoon bridge.* A bridge floating on pontoons which may be unlocked to allow the passage of vessels.
  (6) *suspension.* A bridge on which the roadway is hung from cables anchored over towers without intervening support.

BRIEF. (1) A writ; also a concise statement of a client's case. (2) A statement of the points of a legal argument.

BRITISH THERMAL UNIT (BTU). (1) A standard measurement of heat equal to 252 calories. (2) The quantity of heat required to raise the temperature of one pound of water one degree Fahrenheit at or near its point of maximum density.

BROADLOOM. Carpet woven in widths of 6 to 18 feet.

BROKER. (1) One who buys or sells on commission. (2) A real estate broker is an "agent," as distinguished from a "salesman." A salesman must serve an apprenticeship under a broker for a specified period of time before he may become a real estate *broker.*

BRONZE. An alloy of copper and tin.

BROWN COAL. Lignite: a noncoking mineral usually midway between peat and bituminous coal.

BRUSH. Trees less than four inches in diameter at the stump.

BUDDLE. An inclined, shallow trough for separating ores in running water.

BUFFER ZONE. An area (usually a "green belt") separating housing developments from other activities such as commercial or industrial operations.

BUILDING CODE. (1) Specific type, size, and strength of all building materials and uses thereof are regulated under a building code. (2) The *building code* is usually included with the zoning code regulations.

BULKHEAD. (1) A projecting frame with a sloping roof giving access to a cellar stairway, etc. (2) A small structure on top of a building to cover an elevator shaft. (3) The partition between sections of a vessel.

BULK SHIPMENT. Uncrated or uncontainerized frieght such as sand, cement, coal, and the like.

BULLA. An official seal attached to a document.

BULLDOZER. A heavy piece of equipment with forward blade for pushing dirt and other debris during clearing and grading operations.

BULWARK. (1) Any safeguard or defense. (2) Rampart, parapet, etc.

BUMBOAT. A boat used for peddling provisions to offshore vessels.

BUNA. A synthetic rubber.

BUNKER. A large bin used for storing bulk materials.

BUNT. The bellying part of a square sail.

BURGESS. A citizen or officer of a borough; a burgher.

BURLEY. A thin-bodied light tobacco grown in Kentucky and neighboring states.

BURNETT PROCESS. Full-cell pressure treatment of wood with a salt preservative.

BUS BAR. A bar of copper or aluminum forming a connection between circuits.

BUS DUCT. An electrical conductor which serves as a connection for two or more electrical circuits.

BUSINESS DEVELOPMENT CORPORATION (BDC). A business financing agency, usually comprising the financial institutions of an area or state, organized for assisting in the financing of industrial concerns which are not able to get such through normal channels. The "risk" is spread among various members of the BDC and interest rates are usually somewhat higher than those charged by the individual institutions.

BUTTE. A steep-sided, flat-topped hill.

BUTTRESS. A structure built against a wall to lend strength to it.

BY-BIDDER. A person who runs up prices for a seller at an auction.

BY- ELECTION. An election held between regular elections to fill a vacancy in an elective office.

BY-LAWS. Laws, subordinate to its constitution, adopted by an organization.

BY-PRODUCTS. Something produced secondarily to the main product of a manufacturing operation. (Sawdust is a *by-product* of a lumber mill.)

BYWORK. Work done during leisure time.

C

CABIN CAR. A railroad caboose.

CABLE-LAID. A cable made up of three 3-stranded ropes or wires twisted together counterclockwise.

CABLE LENGTH. A measurement: U.S., 720 feet; England, 608 feet.

CABLET. (1) A hawser. (2) Cable-laid of less than ten inches in circumference.

CABOOSE. A railroad car usually attached to the rear of a freight train in which the crew rides and observes the train's operations. May also be called: way car, hack, shanty, cabin car, crummy.

CABOTAGE. The restriction of airway transportation within the boundaries of a nation.

CADASTER. A survey or map of the extent, ownership, value, etc., of lands as the basis of taxation.

CADASTRAL. Of or pertaining to the value and ownership of real estate.

CAHIER. A report; proceedings.

CAIN. (1) Barter. (2) Rent or tax paid in produce or livestock.

CAISSON. A watertight chamber used for construction work under water; a cofferdam.

CALENDER. A machine for giving gloss to certain materials such as cloth or paper.

CALLABLE. Subject to demand for presentation of payment.

CALL LOAN. A loan which may be terminated on demand of either party at any time; a demand loan.

CALL MARKET. The market for lending money on call or demand.

CALL MONEY. Money loaned on security or deposited in a bank, subject to demand repayment.

CALL RATE. The interest rate on call or demand loans.

CALORIE. (1) The energy-producing content of foods. (2) A *gram calorie* is the amount of heat required to raise one gram of water 1° Centigrade.

CALX. Chalk or lime.

CAMBER. A slight convexity built into a span or trestle to offset the sag resulting from elastic deflections.

CAMEL. (1) A heavy fender between a ship and wharf. (2) A watertight device attached to a vessel to increase its buoyancy.

CAMELBACK. (1) A railroad locomotive with the engineer's cab in the middle rather than to the rear of the engine. (2) An incurred compound of reclaimed rubber combined with crude rubber used for retreading tires.

CAMION. (1) A low, heavy wagon or dray. (2) A military truck.

CANCEL. To annul.

CANDLE. A unit of luminous intensity equivalent to the intensity of light from a ⅞-inch sperm candle burning at the rate of 120 grams per hour; a *standard candle*. A *foot candle* is a unit of illumination of a surface everywhere one foot from a uniform point source of one *international candle*. An *international candle* is the light emitted by five square millimeters of platinum at the temperature of solidification.

CANNIBALIZATION. (1) The dismantling of machinery or equipment for parts. (2) Removal of machinery and equipment from a building.

CANT HOOK. A wood lever resembling a peavey, but with a blunt toe instead of a sharp spike for moving heavy items such as logs.

CANTILEVER. A projecting beam supported only at one end. A *cantilever bridge* is a span consisting of a long structural member lying across a support arch, the projecting arms in balance.

CANTONMENT. A group of temporary structures used as troop headquarters.

CANVAS. A material used for tarpaulins; a tent material.

CANVASS. A poll of opinions, etc.

CAOUTCHOUC *(koo-chook)*. Crude rubber.

CAPABILITY MARGIN. Surplus in excess of peak use of any item, particularly utilities.

CAPACITANCE. The property of a circuit that allows it to store an electrical charge, measured by the accumulated charge divided by the voltage.

CAPACITY. (1) The quantity of electricity that can be delivered under certain conditions. (2) The capability of sewer or water facilities to deliver certain quantities.

CAPACITY FACTOR (ELECTRIC POWER). The ratio of the average load on equipment for the period of time considered to the capacity rating of the equipment.

CAPACITY PEAKING (ELECTRIC POWER). Generating units which are available to assist in meeting that portion of peak load which is above the base load.

CAPILLARY ACTION. A form of surface tension between those of a liquid and those of a solid causing (when the adhesive force is strong) the liquid to rise above the mean level at points of contact with the solid, as water in a glass tube, etc.

CAPITAL. (1) Financial assets. (2) City in which the seat of government is located. (3) The upper member of a column or pillar.

CAPITAL ACCOUNT. A statement of the value of a business at a given time representing assets minus liabilities.

CAPITAL ASSETS. The total amount of money and property owned.

CAPITAL EXPENDITURE. Money spent or debts incurred for property improvements, including buildings and equipment.

CAPITAL GAIN. Profit from the sale of capital investments including real estate, stock, etc.

CAPITAL GOODS. Goods destined for use in production of consumer goods.

CAPITALIZATION. Long-term debt plus preferred stock plus common stock.

CAPITAL LEVY. A levy on capital in addition to income taxes and other taxes; a general property tax.

CAPITAL STOCK. Corporation ownership certificates.

CAPITATION TAX. A levy placed on each adult. (Formerly a poll tax used as a requirement for voting—now outlawed by the courts.)

CAPITOL. The building at the capital in which governments operate.

CAPSTAN. A cylinder used for hoisting heavy weights, weighing anchor, or tightening mooring lines of a vessel; a winch.

CARAT. A weight of 0.2 grams used in weighing precious stones.

CARBONACEOUS. Of, pertaining to, or yielding carbon.

CARBON BLACK. (1) Lampblack. (2) The fine soot deposited from the smoke of burning gas or oil.

CARBON STEEL. (1) Plain steel. (2) Steel containing only the elements of carbon, manganese, phosphorous, sulfur, and silicon in addition to iron, the properties of which are essentially to the same proportion, or percentage, in the steel.

CARBORUNDUM. An abrasive silicon carbon used in grinding wheels and other abrasives.

CARBOY. A large glass container used especially for packaging corrosive acids.

CARBURET. To combine chemically with carbon.

CARBURIZE. To impregnate the surface of low carbon steel with carbon.

CARDINAL POINTS. The four principal points of the compass.

CAR FLOAT. A flat-bottomed boat equipped with tracks on which railroad cars are moved in inland waterways and harbors.

CARGO. Freight; lading; load.

CARLING. A short timber running lengthwise of a ship.

CARLOAD. The minimum weight required for the application of a *carload rate* (not necessarily a car loaded to capacity).

CAR RETARDER. A braking device, usually power-operated, built into a railroad track to reduce the speed of cars by means of brake shoes, which, when set into a braking position, press against the lower flanges of the railroad car wheels. Retarders are now used in almost all railway classification yards.

CARRICK BITT. A post on a ship's deck which supports the end of a windlass.

CARRIER. A company that transports passengers or freight.

CARRY-ALL. A closed automobile having two facing lengthwise passenger seats, often used for conveying workers to jobs.

CARTAGE. (1) Drayage. (2) Intracity hauling. (3) The charges for such carting services.

CARTOGRAM. A map utilizing dots, shadings, surves, etc., to indicate statistics geographically.

CASCADE. (1) A small waterfall or a series of such. (2) In chemistry, a connecting series of two or more electrolytic cells or tanks which produce a flow of the electrolyte from higher to lower levels. (3) In physics, a successive operation, as cooling a gas by utilizing the effect of the previously expanded gas. (4) In electronics, an arrangement of simple and similar subordinate sections or stages within a complex circuit such that the output of one circuit becomes the input of the next circuit.

CASE HARDEN. To harden by carburizing the surface of the low carbon steel followed by quenching.

CASEMENT. A window sash that opens on hinges.

CASH BASIS. Maintaining an account on a daily income and daily expenditure basis.

CASH DISCOUNT. A lower than usual purchase price allowed for payment within a stipulated period.

CASHIER'S CHECK. A check drawn by a bank's cashier upon the bank's funds but deducted from the depositor's account prior to cashing, thus guaranteeing the payee secure payment.

CASTING. (1) Disposing of excavated material by a single operation. (2) An article formed in a mold, as a *steel casting*.

CAST IRON. Alloys of iron containing 1.7 percent to 4.5 percent carbon as cast and usually not appreciably malleable at any temperature.

CAST STEEL. Any steel made by pouring molten steel into molds.

CASUALTY INSURANCE. Insurance of property against loss, damage, or injury.

CASUS. Case; occurrence; event.

CATACLINAL. Strata running in the direction of the dip of a valley.

CATAMARAN. (1) A boat having two parallel hulls. (2) A raft of logs. (3) A heavy wooden sled. (4) A raft or float consisting of pieces of wood lashed together.

CATCH BASIN. A filter at the entrance to a drain or sewer.

CATCHMENT. The catching or collecting of water or the structure involved in such.

CATCHMENT BASIN. The area drained by a river or river basin.

CATENARY. A system of wires suspended between poles supporting overhead wires, normally energized at 11,000 volts for electric train power.

CATHODE. The negatively-charged electrode which receives electrons from an outside source.

CAVEAT. (1) A caution or warning. (2) A notification given to a court not to do a certain act.

CAVETO. A type of concave molding.

CELOTEX. (1) Acoustical tile. (2) Sound-absorbing and heat-insulating board made by compressing bagasse into sheets. (A trade name.)

CEMENT. (1) *Natural cement.* Finely-pulverized product resulting from calcination of argillaceous limestone at a temperature only sufficiently high to drive off the carbonic acid gases. (2) *Portland cement.* A product obtained by finely pulverizing clinker-produced argillaceous, carbonaceous limestone with the only additive being water and gypsum; a hydraulic cement made by calcining limestone with chalk, mud, etc.

CENOTAPH. A tomb or monument erected to the dead but containing no remains.

CENTARE. One square meter; 1,550 square inches.

CENTERLINE. The center of a highway right-of-way or roadway usually staked out before construction.

CENTIGRADE SCALE. A temperature scale at which the boiling point of water is 100° and the freezing point is 0° (comparable to 212° and 32° respectively on the Fahrenheit scale).

CENTIMETER. One-hundredth of a meter; about 4/10 inch.

CENTRAL BUSINESS DISTRICT (CBD). The downtown (central city) retail and business service area of a community.

CENTRAL TRAFFIC CONTROL (CTC). Railroad trackage over which trains are controlled at a central point by remote switch and signal controls.

CENTRIFUGAL. Radiating.

CENTRIFUGAL FORCE. The inverted reaction by which a body tends to move away from a center about which it revolves.

CENTROID. (1) Center of a square. (2) Intersection of median lines of a triangle.

CERAMAL. Combination of metals with ceramic materials.

CERAMIC. Pertaining to articles made of baked clay.

CERTIFICATE. (1) A document stating fact. (2) A writing made in court and legally authenticated.

CERTIFICATE OF CONVENIENCE. A permit issued by a state which authorizes a utility to engage in business, construct facilities, or perform other services.

CERTIFICATE OF NECESSITY. A document issued by a federal authority certifying that certain facilities are necessary in the interest of national defense, permitting accelerated amortization of the facilities over a stipulated period, usually five years.

CERTIFICATE OF NO DEFENSE. An estoppel certificate by which the mortgagor admits he owes the debt and must pay in full at maturity.

CERTIFIED CHECK. A check guaranteed for payment by the bank on which it is drawn. The amount is held in escrow by the bank from the account of the payer.

CERTIFIED INDUSTRIAL DEVELOPER (CID). A designation accorded to professionals in the field of industrial development who have passed examinations and have met other qualifications required by the American Industrial Development Council.

CERTIORARI. A writ from a superior court to a lower court directing that a certified record of its proceedings in a designated case be sent up to the higher court for review.

CESS POOL. A covered pit for the drainage of sanitary waste.

CHAIN. A measurement of 66 lineal feet.

CHAIN PUMP. A pump that raises water by means of buckets on an "endless" chain.

CHAIN REACTION. A self-sustaining series of fissions in which additional fission is initiated by a neutron from previous fission. This process is the basis for the operation of all nuclear reactions.

CHAMFER. To bevel, flute, or cut a furrow in a material.

CHAMPERTY. An illegal transaction made by a third party with one of the parties to a suit. Usually the third party undertakes to render services with the expectation of receiving a share of the matter for which the suit is initiated.

CHARCOAL. A black, porous substance obtained by the imperfect combustion of organic matter, such as wood, used as fuel.

CHARK. Char; convert into charcoal.

CHATS. Residue remaining after extracting ores from rock.

CHATTEL. Any item of movable or immovable property except real estate.

CHATTEL MORTGAGE. A lien against chattels as security for a loan.

CHAUVINISM. (1) Parochial glorification. (2) Vainglorious patriotism.

CHECKOFF. The collection of union dues by deduction from the pay of each employer, then remitted to the union by the employer.

CHEDDITE. An explosive.

CHILIAD. A period of one thousand years.

CHIME. The edge or rim of a cask.

CHIMNEY POT. A pipe placed at the type of a chimney to improve the draft and prevent smoking.

CHINE. The line of intersection between the sides and bottom of a boat.

CHIPBBOARD. A wall board made from wood chips imbedded in the material usually by chemical or pressure process.

CHORD. A straight line connecting the extremities of an arc.

CHOROGRAPHY. The art of describing or mapping a region or area.

CHUTE. An inclined trough for downward transportation of coal, liquids or other materials from one level to another.

CID (CERTIFIED INDUSTRIAL DEVELOPER). A designation accorded to professionals in the field of industrial development who have passed examinations and have met other qualifications required by the American Industrial Development Council.

CINDER BLOCK. A building block, partially hollow, composed of cinders and concrete.

CIRCA. About; used to designate an approximate date (circa 1974)

CIRCUIT. The entire course traversed by an electric current.

CIRCUIT BREAKER. A device for interrupting a circuit under abnormal conditions such as an overload.

CIRCUIT COURT. A court of law that sits in various districts over which its jurisdiction extends.

CIRCUITOUS ROUTE. An extremely indirect route.

CIRCUMAMBIENT. Encompassing; surrounding.

CIRCUMFERENCE. The perimeter of any area, particularly a circle.

CIRCUMFERENTIAL HIGHWAY. (1) A circum-urban freeway.(2) A highway bypassing and usually surrounding a community.

CIRCUM-URBAN. Surrounding a city or metropolitan area.

CIRCUMVALLATE. To surround with a rampart, levee, or trench.

CIRQUE. A circular valley with precipitous walls.

CISTERN. An artificial reservoir for holding liquids; a tank.

CIVIL RIGHTS. The rights, privileges, and immunities of a citizen.

CLAIM. Rights or title to a property.

CLAIM JUMPER. One who seizes another's claim, especially a mining claim.

CLAM SHELL. A dredging or loading bucket hinged to open and close in the manner of a clam; a clam bucket.

CLAPBOARD. A narrow board having one edge thinner than the opposite for purpose of overlapping.

CLASS ACTION. A legal action taken by one or more parties on behalf of a segment of population or as action against a classification of activity.

CLASSIFICATION YARD. A railroad yard in which railroad cars are grouped in accordance with destination or lading requirements and made ready for proper train movement.

CLASS RATES. Transportation charges per hundredweight for certain classes of frieght not accorded commodity rates and not covered by an "exception to the classification." Class rates normally cover less than carload and less than truckload shipments.

CLAYPAN. The underlying soil made of clay; often referred to as "hard pan."

CLEAN ROOM. A room devoid of dust and other extraneous material, used for research where air purity is essential.

CLEARING. A tract of land cleared of woodland, stumps, and shrubbery.

CLEAR TITLE. A title to property devoid of any blemishes or encumbrances.

CLINOMETER. An instrument for measuring angles of elevation or inclination.

CLOSED CIRCUIT. A circuit through which current flows without interference.

CLOSED CIRCUIT TELEVISION. A private television circuit broadcasting within an operating area and received in another area for purposes of surveillance, inspection, education, or entertainment which cannot be viewed by the public at large.

CLOSED CORPORATION. A business enterprise in which the stock is held by a few persons and not available to outside interests.

CLOSED-END INVESTNENT COMPANY. An investment company that has a set amount of capital stock and issues no new shares.

CLOSED MORTGAGE. A mortgage which cannot be paid off before expiration unless the mortgagee is willing to permit such, usually under penalty.

CLOSED SHOP. An establishment where only union members may be employed.

CLOSING. (1) A complete and final shutdown of an existing business establishment in which all operations have ceased and the company has retired from that particular location and field of production and operation. (2) The exchange of final papers with required payment for the transfer of property or the deed to such.

CLOTURE. A parliamentary device to limit debate or stop filibustering in a legislative body.

CLOUD. An outstanding claim, blemish, or encumbrance which can impair an owner's title (e.g., a judgment or dower right).

CLOVERLEAF INTERCHANGE. An intersection resembling a four-leaf clover in which two highways crossing at different levels are connected by a system of curving ramps.

COAL GAS TAR. Coal tar produced during the manufacture of illuminating gas in retorts.

COALITION. An alliance.

COAL TAR. The nonaqueous portion of the liquid distillate obtained during the carbonization of bituminous coal.

COAXIAL CABLE. A cable consisting of two or more insulated conductors surrounded by a central conductor held in place by insulators.

COCKLE BOAT. A vessel's small rowboat; a dinghy.

CODE. Any system of principles or regulations or laws.

CODICIL. A supplement to a will changing or explaining something in it; an appendix or addition.

CODIFY. To systematize.

COEFFICIENT. A number expressing the amount of change or effect under certain conditions as to temperature, volume, size, etc.

COEVAL. (1) Contemporary.(2) Of the same age of duration.

COFFERDAM. A caisson; a water-tight enclosure from which water is pumped to expose the bed of a stream.

COGNATE. (1) Allied by blood; kindred. (2) Similar. (3) Affiliated.

COGNIZANCE. (1) The judicial hearing of a matter. (2) Knowledge by observation. (3) Acknowledgment.

COGNOVIT. A written acknowledgment by a defendant that the plaintiff's demand is just. Made so as to avoid the expense of contending the point.

COGNOVIT NOTE. A demand or judgment note.

COINSURANCE. (1) Joint insurance with others. (2) A form of insurance in which a property owner insures for a percentage of the total value and becomes his own insurer for the remainder.

COKE. A solid carbonaceous fuel obtained by heating coal in ovens to remove its volatile constitutents.

COKE OVEN TAR. Coal tar produced during the manufacture of coke in by-product ovens.

COL. (1) A depression between two mountains. (2) A pass; gap.

COLD DRAWN. Stretched or drawn while cold, as wire.

COLLABORATE. To work jointly with others.

COLLATERAL. (1) Security for loans. (2) Equity. (3) Any asset that can be readily sold which has been pledged to secure the payment of an obligation.

COLLET. A collar or clamp with jaws to hold a rod; a kind of vise.

COLLIERY. A coal mine.

COLLIGATE. To bring or bind together; to unite.

COLLINEAR. Lying in the same straight line.

COLLOCATE. (1) To place side by side or in definite order. (2) To arrange.

COLLY. Coal dust; soot.

COLONNADE. A series of regularly spaced columns supporting an overhang.

COLUMN. A post; pillar.

COLUMN SPACING. The distance between columns within a building.

COMBUSTION FURNANCE. A heating apparatus for determining the amounts of carbon, sulfur, and other components in a material.

COMMERCIAL BANK. A financial institution whose chief functions are acceptance of demand deposits and making short-term loans.

COMMERCIAL PAPER. Short-term negotiable papers originating in business transactions, such as drafts, notes, etc.

COMMERCIAL PROPERTY. Stores, retail and wholesale establishments, and real estate zoned for such uses.

COMMODITY CHARGE. The charge applied to the total volume of gas used during a billing period.

COMMODITY RATE. A freight charge or rate made for the movement of certain goods, usually in carload or truckload lots. These rates are usually less than a "class" rate for the same kind of goods.

COMMON CARRIER. A transportation company serving the public by transporting passengers and/or freight between points prescribed by state or federal agencies.

COMMON LABOR. Unskilled workers performing elementary tasks.

COMMON LAW. (1) A system based on custom, usage, or precedence rather than codified written laws. (2) The system of laws in a state or nation as distinguished from local regulations or specific application.

COMMON PLEAS COURT. A common law court having original jurisdiction over civil and criminal matters.

COMMON STOCK. Corporation stock which entitles the owner to dividends or a share in the profits of the company only after other obligations have been met and dividends rendered to preferred stockholders.

COMMONWEALTH. The body politic. A state in which the sovereignity is vested in its people. Loosely, any of the United States is a *commonwealth,* however, only four of these are officially so designated: Kentucky, Massachusetts, Pennsylvania, and Virginia.

COMMUNAL. Of or belonging to the community.

COMMUNITY. (1) A group of people living together (commune) or in one location subject to the same laws and having common interests. A *community* may be a neighborhood, a town, city, metropolitan area, a county or region. (2) A group having common interests.

COMMUNITY DEVELOPMENT CORPORATION. A corporation set up in an area to develop economic programs for a community and, in most cases, to provide financial support for such economic development; a local development corporation.

COMPACT. An agreement between two or more parties or entities.

COMPACTION TEST. A test to determine the bearing properties of soils. Usually run prior to establishing locations for buildings, especially factories requiring heavy floor loads or stamping equipment (see Handbook section).

COMPANY UNION. A union composed of workers within one company and having no outside union affiliation.

COMPLEMENT. (1) That which fills up or completes a thing. (2) Something which, when added, may enhance the value of the original. (3) An angle which, when added to another angle, produces a sum of 90 degrees.

COMPONENT. A constitutent part.

COMPOST. A composition or compound.

COMPOSTING. A method of getting rid of organic waste through compaction. Sometimes packaged as fertilizer.

COMPREHENSIVE PLAN. A plan including all facets of programming including land use, capital investments, and socioeconomic factors affecting the economy of an area.

COMPTROLLER. An officer whose duties include checking expenditures; a budget director; controller.

CONCEALED LOSS AND DAMAGE. Loss or damage to goods which cannot be determined until a package is opened and inspected.

CONCENTRATION POINT. A location where small shipments are consolidated into larger shipments destined for a common area.

CONCESSION. A grant by a government of land or property rights to use land or property for a specific purpose.

CONCLAVE. A private meeting or secret assembly.

CONCOMMITANT. Existing or occurring with something else; accompanying.

CONCORD. An agreement; accord.

CONCURRENCE. (1) Agreement; assent; consent. (2) A joint power or clause. (3) The point at which three or more lines meet.

CONDEMNATION. Appropriation of property by use of judicial decree or under right of eminent domain.

CONDOMINIUM. Joint ownership of an apartment building wherein the units are owned separately by individuals and not by a corporation or cooperative. An apartment in such building. A monthly charge is made to each owner for outside maintenance. Other housing such as townhouses or single development houses may also be purchased in similar manner. Sometimes called "housominiums."

CONDUCTION. The transmission of heat, sound, or electricity through matter without the motion of the matter.

CONFERENCE. A formal meeting for discussion of matters cogent to the interest of those in attendance.

CONFLUENCE. A flowing together of two or more streams.

CONFUTE. To prove wrong; confound.

CONGRESS. (1) A formal meeting or conference. (2) The legislative body of the United States of America comprising 100 senators (two from each state) and 435 members of the House of Representatives chosen on the basis of population of the various districts which they represent. Although both senators and representatives are members of the U.S. Congress, only the representatives are referred to as "congressmen."

CONGRUENT. Conforming; agreeing.

CONIFEROUS. Cone-bearing. Typical of evergreens characterized by needle-shaped leaves; softwoods.

CONJOIN. To associate or join together.

CONNATE. Innate; congenital.

CONNECTING CARRIER. Common or contract carriers providing free flow of goods through a common interchange point. A carrier which interchanges with another carrier.

CONSANGUINITY. Relationship resulting from common ancestry.

CONSIDERATION. (1) Value received. (2) Amount paid.

CONSIGNEE. One to whom goods are shipped, delivered, billed.

CONSIGNMENT. (1) Freight shipped to a consignee. (2) Goods furnished *on consignment* to a vendor do not require payment by him until sold to the ultimate consumer.

CONSIGNOR. One who ships goods to a consignee.

CONSOCIATE. Unite; bring into association.

CONSOLIDATED SCHOOL. A school attended by pupils from more than one school district.

CONSORTIUM. (1) A coalition, as of banks or corporations, for ventures requiring large financial resources. (2) Any association formed for pooling resources of any kind. (3) A coalition of educational institutions to furnish knowledge in a variety of subjects; a "brain bank."

CONSTITUENT. (1) A necessary part. (2) A voter; one who is represented by a legislative member. (3) A client. (4) A member.

CONSUMER GOODS. Products for satisfying people's needs rather than for producing services (e.g., food, clothing, etc.).

CONSUMER PRICE INDEX. An index issued by the U.S. Department of Labor as a measure of average changes in the retail prices of goods and services bought by families of wage earners and clerical workers living in the cities. The national index is the U.S. city average based on 56 areas and predicated on the weighted cost of a standard shopping list (see Handbook section).

CONTACTOR. A device for opening and closing an electric circuit repeatedly rather than by hand, as a blinker-light operation.

CONTAINER CAR. A flat top or open-top railroad car on which containerized freight is placed for shipment.

CONTAINERIZATION. (1) Freight shipments by container. (2) A shipping system based upon the use of large cargo containers which may be interchanged between truck, ship, and/or train without rehandling the contents.

CONTERMINOUS. Having a common boundary; coterminous; coextensive.

CONTINGENT LIABILITIES. Additional obligations which may arise and are not specifically spelled out in an agreement.

CONTOUR. The outline of a figure, body, land area.

CONTOUR LINE. A line connecting points that are of the same elevation.

CONTOUR MAP. A map showing topographic configuration by means of contour lines each of which is separated from the next by a definitive distance in elevation or height.

CONTRABAND. Goods declared illegal by law; smuggled goods.

CONTRACLOCKWISE. Counterclockwise. In the direction opposite that followed by the hands of a clock.

CONTRACT. An agreement.

CONTRACT CARRIER. A motor carrier not serving the general public but under contract to a particular shipper or shippers.

CONTRACTOR. One who engages to do certain work or furnish goods or services at fixed and agreed rates.

CONTROLLER. An officer responsible for the fiscal planning of any organization; a budget director; comptroller.

CONTUMACY. Defiance and/or disobedience of authority.

CONUS. Continental United States.

CONVENTIONAL FUELS. Fossil fuels; coal; oil; gas.

CONVEYANCE. The transfer of title to property; also the document testifying to such transfer.

COOPER. A maker and repairer of barrels, casks, and the like.

COOPERATIVE. A joint venture entered into by a number of individuals or groups in which costs and income are shared equally among the participants.

COOPERATIVE APARTMENT. An apartment wherein the buyer does not own his living quarters as he does in a condominium but is a stockholder in the overall property and as such is responsible for the upkeep and retirement of debt for the entire building along with the other stockholders.

COORDINATE. (1) Act in harmonious and reciprocal relations; to bring about such action. (2) Any set of magnitudes by means of which the position of a point is determined with reference to the fixed elements.

COORDINATION. Harmonious; integrated action or interaction.

COPARCENARY. An estate in lands inherited in undivided interest by two or more heirs.

COPARTNER. An equal partner.

COPESTONE. The top stone of a wall or building.

COPING SAW. A narrow-bladed saw for cutting curved pieces of wood.

COPPER BARILLA. Native copper mixed with sandstone.

COPPICE. A thicket; copse.

CORD. A measure of wood equal to 128 cubic feet. (4' x 4' x 8')

CORDON. A horizontal molding as of brick or stone projecting along the face of a building.

CORDWOOD. Firewood or pulpwood cut for stacking in a cord.

CORN BELT. The chief corn-growing states: Illinois, Indiana, Iowa, Kansas, Missouri, Nebraska, and Ohio.

CORNERSTONE. A stone uniting two sides of a building.

CORPORATION. (1) A body recognized by law as an individual entity having its own name and identity. (2) An incorporated community.

CORPORATION LINE. Boundary line of an incorporated community.

CORUNDUM. An aluminum oxide used as an abrasive, and second only to diamonds in hardness; carborundum.

CORVÉE. Forced labor.

COTE. A small shelter for sheep or birds.

COTERMINOUS. Conterminous; having a common boundary; coextensive.

COTTAGE INDUSTRY. Production carried on at home usually with the cooperation and assistance of the entire family.

COULEE. A deep gulch cut by rainstorm or melting snow.

COULOIR. A deep gorge or gully on a mountainside.

COULOMB. The practical unit of quantity in measuring electricity; the amount conveyed by one ampere in one second.

COUNTERPOISE. (1) Counterbalance. (2) To bring to a balance by opposing with equal force or weight.

COUNTING HOUSE. A building or office in which a firm carries on bookkeeping, correspondence, etc.

COUNTY COURT HOUSE. The building in which county governmental business is conducted and within which land and property deeds and records are maintained.

COUNTY SEAT. The community wherein the county court house is situated.

COVENANT. (1) A promise in a formal, sealed instrument such as a deed, mortgage, lease, and the like. (2) A compact.

COVER. Usually referred to as "ground cover"; shrubbery, grass, underbrush, clover, etc.

COVERED HOPPER CAR. A hopper car with permanent roof, hatches, and bottom openings for unloading. Used in transporting cement, sand, and other bulk commodities.

CRAFT UNION. A labor union limited to workers who perform similar work. Sometimes referred to as a "horizontal" union.

CRAMPON. A pair of hooked pieces of iron for raising heavy stones, etc.

CRAWL SPACE. A cramped area into which one must crawl to reach other areas. Such may describe the area below buildings through which utility lines may be placed or threaded.

CREDIT. (1) Value received or transferred from a party. (2) Opposite of debt or debit. (3) Financial reputation; ability to obtain loans or lines of credit.

CREDIT LINE. A listing of those to whom credit is due for work done in a news report, etc. (Not to be confused with "line of credit.")

CREDITOR. One to whom something is owed.

CREDIT UNION. A cooperative group for making loans to its members at a low rate of interest. Source of funds is normally through the deposits of the members and interest on loans.

CRIB. (1) A box or small building for the storage of bulk materials. (2) The space between two adjacent railroad ties.

CRITICAL MASS. The mass of nuclear fuel in a reactor sufficient to maintain chain reaction.

CROP ROTATION. A method of conserving and rejuvenating soil fertility by planting different crops in alternate seasons.

CROSSBEAM. A large girder extending from wall to wall of a building, shed, or other structure.

CROSS-BEDDED. Stratum characterized by subsidiary beds and layers of rocks cutting across the main stratification.

CROSSOVER. Two turnouts with the railroad tracks between the frogs arranged to form a continuous passage between two nearby and generally parallel tracks.

CROSSWALK. A lane marked off for use of pedestrians crossing a street.

CRUCIBLE STEEL. A high-grade steel made by melting wrought iron with ferromanganese or other special steels in crucibles placed in specially designed furnaces.

CRYOGENICS. The branch of physics dealing with low temperatures.

CUBAGE. Area multiplied by height.

CUBBYHOLE. A small enclosed space.

CUBIC CAPACITY. The carrying capacity of a truck or railroad car measured in cubic feet.

CUBIC FOOT. Common measuring capacity of a truck or railroad freight car.

CUL DE SAC. A dead-end street with turn-around area for vehicles.

CULLET. Broken or used glass.

CUMBER. A hindrance or encumbrance.

CUMULATIVE VOTING. A system of voting in which the elector may vote as many times as there are candidates on the ballot, giving his votes to all, several, or to one candidate.

CUPEL. (1) The movable bottom in a silver refining furnace. (2) To separate base metals by refining or subjecting to intense heat.

CUPOLA. (1) A dome. (2) A vaulted structure in foundries for exhausting smoke and gases. (3) An upright cylindrical furnace used for melting cast iron.

CUPULE. A concave or cup-shaped depression.

CURB EXCHANGE. An organization for the sale of securities not listed on regular stock exchanges. (The American Stock Exchange formerly was known as "The Curb.") Present-day vernacular refers to unlisted stocks as "OTC" or "over-the-counter" securities.

CURRENCY. The current medium of exchange; paper money.

CURRENT. (1) Alternating current (AC) periodically reverses its direction of flow, each complete cycle having the same value. This is the current in general household use. (2) Direct current (DC) is a current flowing only in one direction. (3) Up to date; contemporary.

CURRENT ASSETS. Cash, deposits, working funds, temporary cash investments, notes, accounts receivables, materials and supplies, prepayments, property less depreciation, inventories.

CURRENT EXPENSES. Any expense necessary for the regular daily maintenance and operation of business.

CURRENT LIABILITIES. Accounts and notes payable, customer deposits, taxes and accrued interest, declared dividends, matured long-term debt, and interest.

CURTAIN WALL. A wall providing enclosure but giving no structural support.

CURTESY. The right which a husband has in his wife's estate at her death.

CURTILAGE. Area of land occupied by a building, its yard and outbuildings actually enclosed or considered enclosed in the total property.

CURVATURE. (1) The rate of change in the deviation of a given arc from any tangent to it. (2) The degree of curve in a railroad track or highway.

CUSEC. Cubic feet per second.

CUSTOM-BUILT. Built to order.

CUSTOM-MADE. Made to order; custom built.

CUSTOMS. (1) Modes or habits. (2) A tariff or duty upon imports.

CUSTOMS BROKER. A person, who, when the ultimate receiver of import goods is unable to meet and pay duty on the imported products when they arrive in the port area, arranges for customs clearance, pays the duty, and relays the shipment to its final destination for a fee.

CUT AND FILL. Borrow and fill; a method of reducing gradient by cutting high-level areas and filling low-level areas.

CUTBACK. A sharp reduction of production and/or personnel.

CUTOFF. (1) A road or route that cuts across an area. (2) A new channel cut by a river across a bend. (3) A mechanism that stops or cuts off the flow of something, such as liquid, gas, steam, etc.

CUTOVER. Cleared land.

CYBERNETICS. The science that treats of the principle of control and communications as they both apply to the operation of complex machines.

CYCLE. In the one cycle of alternating current (AC) the current goes from zero potential or voltage to a maximum in one direction, back to zero, then to the maximum in the other direction and back again to zero and so on. The number of such complete cycles made each second determines the frequency of the current.

CYCLONE FENCE. Trade name of a chain link fence.

CYMA. A curved molding with partly concave and partly convex profile.

D

DADO. (1) The part of a pedestal immediately above the base. (2) The lower part of an interior wall.

DAIS. A raised platform.

DALLES. (1) Dells. (2) Steep rock walls. (3) Rapids running between steep rock walls.

DAMNIFY. To cause damage or injury.

DANDY ROLL. A cylinder of wire by which paper is given a water mark.

DANK. Cold and damp.

DATA. Facts; information.

DATUM. A fact.

DATUM PLANE. The horizontal plane from which height and depth is measured.

DAVIT. A shipboard crane for hoisting or lowering life boats.

DC, DIRECT CURRENT. A flow of current in only one direction.

DEADHEAD. (1) An employee of a transportation company given free passage. (2) A piece of transportation equipment returning to a point of origin without a return payload.

DEADLOAD. U1) Dead weight. (2) The weight of a permanent load or structure.

DEADMAN. An anchorage for a guy wire or cable, usually buried in the ground.

DEAD WEIGHT. (1) Dead load. (2) An inert, heavy load.

DEARTH. Lack of; shortage.

DEBENTURE. (1) A certificate given as acknowledgment of a debt secured by the general credit of the issuing corporation. (2) A bond, usually without security, issued by a corporation, sometimes convertible to common stock.

DEBENTURE STOCK. A debenture of a corporation or a public body issued in the form of stock, the certificates of which are transferable but not redeemable and entitle the holder to a perpetual annuity.

DECAGON. A ten-sided figure.

DECANT. To pour off.

DECARBONATB. To free from carbon dioxide.

DECARBURIZE. To free from carbon.

DECARE, DEKARE. (1) A measure of volume equal to ten steres. (2) Ten cubic meters; 1,000 square meters. (3) Ten acres. (See Handbook section.)

DECENNARY. (1) A tithing. (2) Pertaining to a ten-year period.

DECENNIUM. A period of ten years; a decade.

DECIBEL. One-tenth of a bel, the common unit of power ratio; a measure of sound intensity.

DECIDUOUS. Falling off, as leaves from certain trees.

DECIMETER. One-tenth of a meter.

DECISTERE. One-tenth of a stere; a cubic decimeter.

DECLARATION. (1) A solemn statement made in lieu of an oath. (2) The written statement of a plaintiff's causes and claims.

DECLINE. Decrease in value.

DECLIVITY. A downward slope or descending surface.

DECOCT. (1) To extract by boiling. (2) Condense.

DECORTICATE. To peel, especially the bark from a tree.

DECREPITATE. To heat a material (especially minerals) so as to make a cracking sound.

DEDICATED STREET. A right-of-way donated to a governmental subdivision by the rightful owner in order to get street access.

DEDICATION. (1) A setting aside of an area. (2) To open or unveil. (3) An appropriation of land by an owner to some public use, with acceptance for such use by a public body.

DEED. Any written, sealed instrument of bond, contract, or transfer, especially of real estate.

DEED OF TRUST. A written instrument wherein a property owner pledges his property by conveying title to one or more trustees.

DE FACTO. Actually existing.

DEFAULT. Failure to meet an obligation when due.

DEFEASANCE CLAUSE. An instrument or clause nullifying the effect of some other action; making null and void.

DEFEASIBLE. Capable of being rendered null and void.

DEFICIENCY JUDGMENT. The difference between the indebtedness sued for and the sale price of the real estate or property at a foreclosure sale.

DEFICIT. (1) A lack of funds sufficient to balance accounts. (2) A condition in which expenditures exceed income.

DE FORCE. To prevent by force from obtaining lawful possession.

DEGREE DAY. A unit representing a declination of the mean outside temperature from the standard temperature of 65° Fahrenheit, used to determine fuel requirements for heating a building.

DEGREE OF CURVE. The angle subtended at the center of a simple curve by a 100-foot cord.

DEHUMIDIFY. Remove moisture.

DEHYDRATE. Remove or deprive of water.

DE JURE. By right; legally.

DELICT. A misdemeanor; tort; crime.

DELIMIT. To bound; prescribe the limits of.

DELINEATE. Describe.

DELIVERY. Transfer of a deed.

DEMAND. The rate at which electric energy is delivered to or by a system of piece of equipment expressed in kilowatts or kilovolt amperes or other unit at a given instant, as averaged over a period of time.

DEMANDANT. Plaintiff.

DEMAND CHARGE. The charge specified in the rate applied to the volume of gas.

DEMAND FACTOR. The ratio of the maximum demand over a specified time period to the total connected load on any defined system.

DEMAND NOTE. (1) Demand load. (2) A promissory note payable on demand.

DEMESNE. The grounds belonging to any residence or landed estate; domain.

DEMOGRAPHY. The study of vital and social statistics.

DEMURRAGE. (1) The detention of any vessel, railroad freight car or other commercial conveyance beyond the specified time for departure. (2) A penalty charged to the shipper or receiver of goods for such detention.

DEMURRER. A pleading that allows the truth of the facts stated by the opposing party, but denies that they are sufficient cause to constitute reason for action or defense in law.

DENARY. (1) Containing or composed of ten. (2) Preceding by ten.

DENATURED ALCOHOL. Alcohol made unfit for human consumption by adding poisonous substances.

DENE. A sandy stretch of land, or low sandy hill, near the sea.

DENUDATION. (1) The laying bare of land by erosion. (2) The slow distintegration of rock surfaces caused by weathering.

DEPLETION ALLOWANCE. A charge against income for the pro rata cost of the extracted depletable resources.

DEPRECIATION. Loss in value or efficiency resulting from age, deterioration, usage, etc.; functional or economic obsolescence.

DESCRIPTIVE LISTING. A presentation of facts concerning real estate, including location, size, boundaries, improvements, accouterments, ownership, zoning, price, etc.

DESICCATOR. An apparatus for drying meal, vegetables, etc., as well as for absorbing moisture from chemicals.

DESIGNEE. A person who has been designated or appointed.

DESPOIL. To strip or deprive of possession.

DESSIATINE. A unit of area amounting to 2.698 acres (Russian).

DETERMINANT. That which determines. In mathematics, a numerical value assigned to a square matrix.

DETONATE. To cause to explode.

DEVELOPMENT. (1) A tract of land served with utilities and other facilities such as road access. (2) A group of similarly designed houses usually constructed by one builder. (3) A subdivision.

DEVELOPMENT DISTRICT. A group of counties having common geographic, social, and economic ties and facing interrelated development problems. The district serves as a regional clearing house for most federal and state grant-in-aid programs.

DEVEST. To take away as an estate.

DEVIL'S ADVOCATE. One who, for the sake of debate, takes the unfavorable side in discussion or argument.

DEVISE. To bequeath.

DEVOLVE. To pass on to a successor.

DEW POINT. The temperature at which dew forms or condensation of vapor occurs.

DEXTRAL. Turned toward the right.

DEXTRAN. A white, gum-like substance produced by bacterial action in milk, molasses, etc.

DEXTRIN. A gummy water-soluble substance formed by the action of acids or heat and used as a substitute for gum arabic and used in medicines, candy, etc.

DIAMOND INTERCHANGE. An intersection resembling a diamond in which two highways crossing at different levels are connected by direct ramps. Usually constructed at intersections with secondary traffic on one of the roads or where topography limits construction of a cloverleaf interchange.

DICHOTOMY. Verbal interchange between two parties representing opposing views from which compromise may be achieved.

DICTUM. A positive, authoritative pronouncement.

DIE. Any of various hard metal devices for stamping, shaping, or cutting.

DIELECTRIC. Nonconducting, therefore capable of sustaining an electric field.

DIESEL ENGINE. An internal combustion engine in which air without fuel is compressed in the cylinder to a pressure of about 500 psi at which its temperature is about 1100° Fahrenheit. At this temperature, fuel injected near the end of the compression stroke ignites and burns during the early part of the power stroke, ideally maintaining a uniform pressure as the gases expand against the moving piston until combustion is completed.

DIFFERENTIAL ROUTE. A route for which the rate must be calculated by adding and/or subtracting a differential rate from a through rate. In other words, a transportation route for which there is no published rate so that the freight rate must be computed by a combination of existing published rates.

DIKE. (1) A levee. (2) A mass of igneous rock intruded into a fissure in other rocks.

DILUVIAL. Pertaining to flood.

DILUVIUM. Coarse rock material transported and deposited by glaciers; glacial drift.

DIODE. An electron tube or semiconductor device having two terminals and, in addition to other properties, which can act as a rectifier.

DIRECT CURRENT (DC). An electric current flowing in one direction.

DIRECT TAX. A tax placed on income, property, etc., that is charged directly to the taxpayer and cannot be passed on to another.

DISCIPLINE. A branch of knowledge or instruction.

DISCLAIMER. (1) Disavowal. (2) A repudiation of a legal claim.

DISCOUNT. (1) Deduction for interest at the time of making a loan. (2) A loan on notes, accounts receivables, etc., at a rate less than the face value. (3) Below the regularly charged amount. (4) A deduction for paying a debt within a stipulated period.

DISCRETE. A separate entity; individually distinct.

DISENTAIL. To free an estate.

DISPOSSESS. (1) To oust; evict. (2) To deprive of use.

DISTAFF. The female side; women in general.

DISTAFF SIDE. The maternal or female line of the family.

DISTRAIN. To seize and detain personal property as security.

DISTRIBUTION WAREHOUSE. A structure utilized for the temporary storage of goods and the distribution of such to customers.

DIVINING ROD. A device which it is alleged can, if held correctly, point down to where underground water may be found.

DOCK. A wharf; pier.

DOCKAGE. (1) The facilities for docking or mooring a vessel. (2) The charges for docking a vessel.

DOCKWALLOPER. One who handles freight on a dock; a stevadore.

DOCUMENTED. (1) Attested to. (2) Certified by the Maritime Inspection Service as having been constructed in the United States.

DOLLY. A small-wheeled conveyance for moving goods.

DOLOMITE. High-grade limestone sometimes resembling marble.

DOMAIN. (1) Realm. (2) A sphere or field of action or interest.

DOMESTIC. Produced or existing within a country.

DORIC. Of or pertaining to the simplest of Greek architecture.

DOSIMETER. An instrument for measuring the total amount of radiation absorbed by a person in a given time.

DOSSIER. A collection of documents relating to a particular matter or person.

DOT. Dowry.

DOTATION. Endowment.

DOUBLE ENTRY. A method of bookkeeping in which every transaction is made to appear as both a debit and a credit.

DOUSE, DOWSE. Search for underground water with a divining rod.

DOWAGER. In English law, a widow holding property or title from her pre-deceased husband.

DOWEL. A pin or peg fitted into adjacent holes of two pieces in order to hold them tightly together.

DOWER. The part of a deceased man's estate that is assigned by law to his widow for life.

DRAFT. (1) An order to pay money. (2) A rough outline.

DRAINAGE BASIN. (1) An area or district drained by topography to a stream or body of water. (2) The area into which several streams drain.

DRAW. A gully or ravine into which water drains.

DRAWING ACCOUNT. An account from which one may draw expenses or cash advances against anticipated income from commissions.

DRAYAGE. Charges made for the delivery of goods hauled from a terminal or warehouse to a consignee's door.

DREDGE. A large scoop or suction device for deepening channels.

DRIFT. A horizontal passage in a mine.

DRILL TRACK. A railroad track connecting with the ladder track over which locomotives and cars may move in switching within a classification yard.

DROP. The vertical distance between one level and another.

DROP FORGER. A machine employing the mechanical force of a dropped weight in order to forge metals.

DROSS. Refuse or impurity in metal; slag; cinders.

DROVER. (1) One who drives animals to market. (2) A dealer in such.

DRUMLIN. A mound of unstratified glacial debris; drum.

DRY DOCK. A floating or stationary structure from which water can be removed, used for building, repairing, and refurbishing ships.

DRY KILN. A heated oven or chamber in which lumber may be dried or seasoned.

DUCT. Any passage by which fluid or gas is transported.

DUCTILITY. The physical property of a material which permits permanent distortion without rupture.

DUNE. A hill of loose sand.

DUNNAGE. Material used to protect or support freight, such as bracing, racks, props, etc.

DUPLEX. A single, two-story structure designed for two-family occupancy.

DUPLEX APARTMENT. In the U.S., an apartment having rooms on two floors. (2) In Canada, a two-story building having an apartment on each floor.

DURESS. (1) Constraint by fear, force, compulsion. (2) A coercion to do or say something against one's will or judgment.

DUTY. A tax or tariff on imported goods.

DYNAMITE. An explosive composed of nitrogylcerine held in some absorbent subject.

DYNAMO. A generator for the conversion of mechanical energy into electrical energy through the agency of electromagnetic induction.

E

EARNED INCOME. Income from labor, business transactions or other activites in which personal effort of the recipient is involved.

EARNEST MONEY. (1) Money paid in advance to bind a contract. (2) Good faith deposit.

EARNINGS PRICE RATIO. Earnings per share on common stock divided by its market price per share.

EARTH BORER. An auger for boring into the ground; often used in mining operations.

EASEMENT. The privilege or right of making limited use of another's property such as the *easement rights* granting an electric power company access to cross a property with power lines and permitting entry for the maintenance thereof.

EASTERLY. (1) An *easterly wind* is a wind blowing from the east. (2) An *easterly movement* or *easterly direction* is toward the east.

ECLECTIC. Favoring no particular belief or practice but selecting from all methods.

ECOLOGY. (1) The study of the environment. (2) Bionomics.

ECONOMIC DETERMINISM. The theory that all human activities and institutions have economic origins.

ECONOMIC DEVELOPMENT DISTRICT. A development district; a group of counties having common geographic, social, and economic ties and facing interrelated development problems. The district serves as a regional clearing house for most federal and state grant-in-aid programs.

ECONOMIC DEVELOPMENT FACTORS (PIE). The factors affected by federal assistance are usually referred to as "PIE": Popoulation, Investment, Employment.

ECONOMIC GEOGRAPHY. The division of geography which deals with the realtionship between natural resources and human economic activity.

ECONOMIC LIFE. The period over which property may be profitably utilized.

ECOTONE. The transition area between two communities.

ECUMENICAL. (1) Worldwide. (2) Universal.

EFFLUVIUM. Foul-smelling exhalation from decaying materials.

EFFLUX. A flowing out; emanation.

EFFUSE. (1) To spread, out loosely or flat. (2) To exude.

EGALITARIAN. Relating to political and social equality.

EJECTMENT. A form or action to regain possession of real property.

ELECTRIC ENERGY. Kilowatt hours.

ELECTRIC FURNACE PROCESS. The method of making steel from scrap or steel scrap and iron ore with limestone as the flux in the furnace, usually of the rocking or tilting type, in which the source of heat is a low voltage electric current of high amperage.

ELECTRODE. Any terminal connecting a conventional conductor.

ELECTROGRAPH. An apparatus for tracing a design on metal plates to be used in pattern printing, such as wallpaper, etc.

ELECTROKINETICS. The science dealing with the motion of charged particles.

ELECTROLYSIS. The application of direct current to an electrolyte so as to attract its positive ions to the cathode and its negative ions to the anode.

ELECTROLYTE. A chemical solution that conducts electricity.

ELECTROMAGNET. A material which becomes a temporary magnet during the passage of an electric current through a coil of wire surrounding it.

ELECTROMETALLURGY. The conduct of metallurgical operations by means of electricity.

ELECTRON. An atomic particle carrying a unit charge of negative electricity (1/1837 of a proton).

ELECTRONICS. The branch of engineering that deals with the design and production of such appliances and devices as radios, TV sets, computers, etc., that contain electron tubes, transistors, or related components.

ELEEMOSYNARY. Pertaining to charity.

ELEGANT. (1) Marked by ingenuity and simplicity. (2) In economics, and *elegant* solution.

ELEMENTARY EDUCATION. Education preceding secondary school: the first six (or eight) grades of school preceding high (or junior high) school.

ELEVATION. (1) In drafting: a view of a machine or other structure from side, front, or rear or a drawing depicting such. (2) In surveying, the distance from ground level to the top of a building, tract of land, etc.

ELL. A room or extention to a house built at right angles to the original structure.

ELUTRIATE. To purify or separate by washing, straining, or decanting.

ELUVIUM. A deposit of soil and dust particles remaining where they were formed by the decomposition of rock masses.

EMBARGO. Authoritative stoppage of any special trade or goods.

EMBOUCHURE. The mouth of a river.

EMBRACERY. The act of corruptly influencing or attempting to influence a jury, commission, judge, etc.

EMENDATION. A correction or improvement, particularly a text.

EMINENT DOMAIN. The right or power of a government to take private property for public use, usually at adequate compensation.

EMPIRICAL. (1) Relating to, or based upon, direct experience or observation alone. (2) Relying on practical experience without benefit of scientific knowledge or theory.

ENACT. Make into law.

ENCHIRDION. A handbook; manual.

ENCLAVE. A district, as in a city, inhabited by a minority group; a ghetto.

ENCROACHMENT. A building or part thereof intruding upon the property of another.

ENCUMBRANCE. A lien or claim against real property; anything that precludes against clear title to a property.

ENDEMIC. Native to an area, such as plants, animals, etc.

ENDORSEMENT IN BLANK. An endorsement on a negotiable instrument that names no payee, making it payable to the bearer.

ENERGETICS. The science of the laws and phenomena of energy.

ENNEAD. Any system or group containing nine.

ENTABLATURE. The uppermost member of a column or pillar.

ENTENTE. A mutual agreement and the parties thereto.

ENTRÊPOT. A storage place for commercial wares.

ENTREPRENEUR. One who undertakes to start and conduct an enterprise assuming full control and risk.

ENTRESOL. A mezzanine just above the ground floor of a building.

ENVIRONMENT. The aggregate of external circumstances that affect the existence and development of an area or social unit.

EPITOME. (1) A typical example. (2) An extreme example. (3) A concise summary. (4) The most, or best.

EQUAL-AREA. (Of map projections) Maintaining a constant relationship between a unit area of the map and the corresponding area of the earth regardless of location (e.g., one inch equals one mile).

EQUIPMENT. (1) The rolling stock of a transportation company. (2) Office machines—typewriters, computers, etc.—as differentiated from production machinery.

EQUITABLE. Valid in equity (as distinguished from statute).

EQUITY. The net interest which an owner has in a property.

EQUITY CAPITAL. The portion of the total capital furnished by stockholders or owners as opposed to borrowed capital.

EQUITY FINANCING. Capital raised through the sale of stock.

EQUITY OF REDEMPTION. The right according a mortgagor to redeem his mortgaged property on payment of the sum due even though the time appointed for payment has passed.

EROSION. The wearing away of land by stream, wind, precipitation.

ERRATUM. An error in writing or printing.

ESCALATOR CLAUSE. A clause in a contract or lease permitting increases in charges under certain agreed upon conditions.

ESCARPMENT. (1) A steep slope. (2) An artificial, precipitous slope such as around a fortification or in highway construction through mountainous areas.

ESCHEAT. Reversion of property to the state in default of legal heirs.

ESCROW. (1) A written contract placed in the custody of a third party and effective when delivered by the third party to the grantee upon fulfillment of stipulated ccnditions. (2) Funds held in *escrow* by a third party as evidence of earnest intent to fulfill all obligations agreed to by the grantors and grantees.

ESKER. A ridge of stratified sand and gravel deposited by glacial action.

ESOTERIC. (1) Obscure; lying beyond normal comprehension. (2) Understood by, or meant only for, a few instructed individuals.

ESPLANADE. A level open stretch used as a roadway or public promenade.

ESPOUSE. To support, promote.

ESTATE. (1) The degree, nature, and extent of interest to which one is lawfully entitled with regard to the ownership or use of property; rights of ownership or disposal. (2) The property under ownership.

ESTATE IN REVERSION. The residue of an estate left in the grantor to commence in possession after terminating of some particular estate granted by him. (In lease, the lessor has the *estate in reversion* after termination of the lease.)

ESTOP. Check or bar by estoppel proceedings.

ESTOPPEL. An impediment to a right of action whereby one is forbidden to deny one's previous act or statement.

ESTOVERS. Necessary supplies allowed by law (e.g., wood for a tenant; alimony for an ex-spouse).

ESTREAT. (1) A true copy of an original record. (2) To take by way of levy, fine, etc.

ESTUARY. Wide mouth of a river where its current is met by the sea and is influenced by tides.

ETAPE. A public warehouse.

ET UX. And wife.

EUGENICS. The science of the physical and mental qualities of human beings through control of the fact influencing heredity or by selecting a parent(s).

EUROPEAN ECONOMIC COMMUNITY (EEC). (1) A customs union of certain European nations including France, Italy, West Germany, Benelux, and Great Britain. (2) The Common Market.

EUROPEAN PLAN. The system of paying for room apart from meal charges; the oposite of the American plan.

EUROPEAN RECOVERY PLAN (ERP). (1) The Marshall Plan. (2) Assistance program of the United States to aid the European nations in recovering economically from World War II through financial and technical assistance.

EUTHENICS. The science of improving the physical and mental qualities of human beings through control of environmental factors.

EVALUATION. Market or other value of property. Assessed evaluation is that valuation set by law of property which has been so assessed and on which the taxes forthcoming are set.

EVICTION. (1) Expulsion of a tenant by due legal process.

EXACT SCIENCE. A Science the data of which are predictable on the basis of quantitative laws.

EXCESS PROPERTY. Property no longer required by a federal agency for its needs or discharge of its responsibilities. The property becomes *excess* after it has been determined that there is no further use for it within the "holding" agency. It may then be reassigned to another federal agency.

EXCISE TAX. An indirect tax on certain commodities assessed by a unit of government (e.g., taxes on liquor, tobacco, etc.).

EXCITATION. The power required to energize the magnetic field of generators in an electric generating station.

EXCLAVE. A minor portion of a country separated from the main part and lying in an "alien" territory.

EXCLUSIVE LISTING. A listing of real property through one realtor as sole agent for a designated period of time.

EXECUTED. (1) Finished. (2) Accomplished in legal form.

EXECUTOR. One who is appointed by the testator to carry out the terms of a wl after the testator's death. (feminine: executrix).

EXEMPLI GRATIA (e.g.). For example.

EXEMPT CARRIER. Trucks hauling certain commodities are exempt from Interstate Commerce Commission economic regulation. The majority of *exempt carriers* transport perishable food products.

EXEQUATUR. In international law, the official recognition given a consul or commercial agent by the government of the nation to which he has been assigned.

EXHIBIT. (1) A document or other object formally submitted to a court or officer as a piece of evidence. (2) Supporting documents to research studies, etc.

EXIGENT. Urgent; demanding.

EXPANSION. An added operation by an existing company in an addition built contiguous to its existing facilities or in another building (new or existing) in the same community.

EX PARTE. From, or in the interest of, one side only; one-sided.

EXPEDITE. To accelerate; speed up.

EXPERTISE. Know-how; knowledgeability; expertness.

EXPLICIT. Plainly expressed; developed in detail and free from obscurity, not merely implied.

EXPRESSAGE. (1) The transportation of goods by express or expedited service. (2) The amount charged for such.

EXPRESSWAY. A highway designed for high-speed motor vehicle transportation.

EXPROPRIATION. The taking of property from an owner, especially for public use by right of eminent domain. To deprive one of ownership.

EXTANT. Still existing; surviving; not destroyed.

EXTENSION COURSE. Studies offered to individuals not enrolled in the regular student body; adult or evening courses.

EXTENSION SERVICE. Services offered by institutions of learning, sometimes in cooperation with the U.S. Department of Agriculture, and directed toward improving and assisting the growth of agricultural products. (This service will be especially active in programs under the Rural Development Act.)

EXTRACTIVE INDUSTRIES. Those industries utilizing natural resources (e.g., mining, forestry, gas and petroleum products, etc.).

EXTRADOS. The outer, or convex, surface of an arch.

EXTRA HIGH VOLTAGE (EHV). (1) Voltage levels of transmission lines above normal levels. (2) 345,000 volts and higher.

EXTRAPOLATE. To project those values of a magnitude or function that lie beyond the range of known values on the basis of values that have already been determined.

EXURBIA. The area beyond the suburbs.

F

FABRICATION-IN-TRANSIT. A freight rate permitting shipment from point A to point B at which latter point some fabrication is permitted and the shipment then continues to final destination point C. The applicable rate is the through rate from A to C on the final commodity. This rate is usually less than the combination of rates from A to B, plus B to C.

FACADE. The front or principal face of a building.

FACEPLATE. A disc that holds and rotates work, as on a lathe.

FACTOR. (1) One who transacts business for another on a commission basis. (2) A person or organization that undertakes to finance the operations of certain companies, accepting accounts receivable as collateral.

FACTORAGE. The business of a factor or his commission.

FACTORING. Selling accounts receivable to a factor on a continuing basis. More about *factoring* and how it works:

(1) As orders are received from customers, the vendor sends them to the factor for approval of credit.
(2) Upon receiving credit approval, shipments are made and sales invoices are sent to the factor.
(3) The factor advances cash to the vendor on the basis of total invoice amounts less a percentage fee charged to the vendor by the factor.
(4) The factor then is responsible for collections and the bookkeeping involved.

An example of a type of factoring is the business carried on by credit card companies who bill the consumer directly, but usually make immediate payment to the vendor. *Maturity factoring* differs from the above described method in that the factor pays the vendor on the maturity dates of receivables whether or not the customer pays promptly.

FACTORIZE. To garnishee.

FAILURE. Bankruptcy.

FAIR COPY. A copy of a document after final correction.

FAIR MARKET VALUE. The price of a product agreed upon by a seller and buyer, neither of whom are under any compulsion to either buy or sell the property under consideration.

FAIR TRADE. To set a price no less than the minimum price allowed on a branded product by a manufacturer.

FAIRWAY. That portion of a harbor through which ships pass to and from the open sea.

FALL LINE. The beginning of a plateau as indicated by waterfalls and rapids.

FALLOW. (1) Uncultivated land. (2) To leave unseeded after plowing.

FARAD. The unit of capacitance. The capacitance of a condenser that retains one coulomb of charge with one volt of difference of potential.

FARMSTEAD. A farm and the buildings thereon.

FASCINE. Brush or scrub bound in bundles to protect a river bank.

FATHOM. A measure of length equal to six feet (1.829 meters).

FATIGUE. Structural weakness or loss of resiliency in metals caused by excessive or repeated strain.

FEASIBLE. Practical; suitable.

FEASIBILITY STUDY. (1) A study to determine the profitability of a projected program or operation. (2) An analysis of factors which a company would include in its requirements. (3) The examination of a specific situation.

FEATHERBEDDING. (1) The practice of requiring employment of more workers than are actually required. (2) Artificially limiting output so as to create more jobs.

FEDERAL RESERVE SYSTEM. A twelve-district operation with twelve Federal Reserve designed to regulate and aid member banks within the districts.

FEE. (1) Payment. (2) Charge. (3) Gratuity.

FEEDER. (1) An electric line for supplying electric energy within an electric service area or subarea. (2) A subsidiary transportation company bringing freight from "remote" areas to the main line of a trunk trasportation company.

FEEDER STOCK. Livestock being fed and fattened for shipment to processing and packing plants.

FEE SIMPLE. (1) Complete ownership. (2) An estate of land inherited without any restrictions.

FELDSPAR. A crystalline rock that consists of aluminum silicates with other materials.

FEN. Marsh; swamp; bog.

FENESTELLA. A small window.

FERROUS. Of or pertaining to iron.

FERRULE. A metal ring used near the end of a shaft to protect the end or reinforce the shaft.

FERRUM. Iron.

FIAR. One in whom the fee simple of an estate is vested.

FIAT. An authorizational decree.

FIAT MONEY. Paper tender made legal by decree; not based on gold or silver reserves nor necessarily convertible to coins; scrip.

FID. A square bar used to support a top mast of a vessel.

FIDEJUSSION. The condition of being bound as surety for another.

FIDUCIAL. Based on trust.

FIDUCIARY. (1) Pertaining to or acting as trustee. (2) Held in trust (as a *fiduciary estate*.) (3) Consisting of fiat money.

FIELD MAGNET. The magnet that produces the magnetic field in a motor or generator.

FIERI FACIAS. A writ of execution commanding a sheriff to levy on goods of a debtor to satisfy a judgment.

FIFTH WHEEL. Device used to connect a tractor to a semitrailer.

FILIBUSTER. Dilatory tactic, usually in the form of long-winded speeches on a variety of nonrelevant a subjects, designed to prevent a vote on a legislative action or bill.

FILL BENCH. A man-made slope created by pushing or bulldozing debris down a hill.

FINANCE BILL. Legislation to raise money for government use.

FINDER'S FEE. A fee charged an agent to a client for obtaining customers, financing, or other services.

FINITE. Limited; having bounds.

FIORD, FJORD. A narrow arm of the sea running between high, rocky cliffs or banks.

FIREBREAK. A strip of land which has been cleared to prevent the spread of fire.

FIREGUARD. (1) A firebreak. (2) A fire screen.

FIREPROOF. Resistant to fire and virtually incombustible.

FIRE RESISTANT. Not completely fireproof, but delaying the spread of a fire.

FIREWALL. A fireproof wall designed to block a fire's progress; a bulkhead.

FIRM. (1) A business concern. (2) Partners and employees of a business taken collectively.

FIRM POWER. Power intended to be available at all times during the period covered by a commitment, even under adverse conditions.

FIRN. Granular snow.

FIRST MORTGAGE. A mortgage having priority over all other mortgages.

FIRTH. (1) A narrow arm of the sea. (2) The opening of a river into the sea.

FISCAL. Financial.

FISCAL YEAR. The period of twelve months covered in a budget of a company which may commence in any month of the year, unlike a *calendar year* which always starts January 1.

FISSILE. Capable of being split or separated into layers.

FISSION. (1) The act of splitting apart. (2) The disintegration of the nucleus of an atom.

FISSURE. A narrow opening or cleft.

FIT RAIL. Used railroad track determined by inspection to be satisfactory or *fit* for construction of industrial tracks.

FIXED ASSETS. Property; personal and real.

FIXED CHARGES. Charges that cannot be readily changed or avoided such as rent, insurance, interest, depreciation, taxes, etc.

FIXTURES. Any chattel or article of personal property annexed or affixed to realty with intent that it becomes a part thereof and that, as thereafter governed by law, becomes real property.

FLAG STATION. (1) A railroad station at which a train stops only on signal. (2) A flag stop.

FLAMMABLE. Easily ignited.

FLASHBOARD. A board set at the top or side of a dam to prevent flash flooding.

FLATCAR. A railroad car without sides or roof used principally for hauling lumber, heavy machinery, steel bars, etc.

FLINT GLASS. Clear, or "white" glass.

FLOATATION. The act of financing a business by issuing bonds.

FLOAT BRIDGE. A structure with an adjustable apron to connect railroad tracks on land with those on a car float or lighter.

FLOAT GLASS. A process developed in England in which a continuous ribbon of top-grade glass is produced by passing molten glass over an enclosed bath of molten tin. The temperature is gradually reduced as the glass hardens thus taking on the flatness of the molten tin. Most automotive glass is of this type. In order to produce float glass, an especially long, narrow building is required.

FLOATING ZONE. A particular district or category of land use is set out in a zoning ordinance but no area of land is found or so designated on the zoning map.

FLOODGATE. A gate at the head of a water channel designed to regulate the flow and/or depth of the water in the channel.

FLOODPLAIN. A plain or area bordering a stream which is subject to flooding and in which area certain activities are barred through *floodplain zoning restrictions*.

FLOOD RECORD. A recording of frequency, dates, duration, and highwater marks of flooding in an area.

FLOODWALL. A wall designed to prevent flooding of an area. Some of these walls are movable so as to allow highway traffic in an area during nonflood periods.

FLOTAGE. The part of a ship's hull above the water line.

FLOTSAM. Objects floating on a body of water.

FLOWING WELL. An artesian well in which the pressure causes water to rise above the surface of the ground.

FLUVIAL. Pertaining to, found in, or formed by a river.

FLUX. A substance that promotes the fusing of metals, such as borax or limestone.

FOLLOWER. A member interposed between the hammer and a pile to transmit blows from a pile driver to a pile.

FOOTCANDLE. The illumination thrown on one square foot of surface, all points of which are one foot from one international candle.

FOOTING. (1) A footer. (2) A structural unit used to distribute wall or column loads to foundation materials.

FOOT-POUND. A unit of measurement of energy expended based on the amount of energy necessary to raise one pound mass one linear foot.

FORCED SALE. (1) A foreclosure. (2) Sale of personalty, realty, etc., under complusion in order to satisfy outstanding debts.

FORECLOSE. (1) To deprive a mortgagor in default of the right to redeem a mortgaged property. (2) To take away the power to redeem a mortgage or pledge.

FOREIGN BILL. A bill of exchange drawn in one country and made payable in another.

FOREIGN EXCHANGE. (1) The transaction of monetary affairs between parties of one country and those of another. (2) Bills of exchange drawn in one country and payable in another.

FOREIGN-TRADE ZONE. The whole or part of a port area where no customs or duties are levied on foreign goods until such time as such goods move out into the country of destination.

FORESHORE. Land between high and low water marks.

FORFEITURE. The giving up or loss of something by way of penalty.

FORGE. An apparatus used for heating and softening metal to be worked into shape, as by hammering.

FOREJUDGE. To deprive, as of a right, by judgment of the court.

FORKLIFT. A motorized mobile machine to move and stack goods loaded on pallets or skids.

FOUNDATION. (1) That part of a building wholly or partly below the surface of the ground that constitutes the base. (2) An endowment or an endowed institution that grants funds for or conducts research or support projects.

FOUNDATION BED. The surface on which a structure rests.

FOURTH SECTION. This is a section of the Interstate Commerce Act prohibiting railroads from charging more for a short haul than for a longer haul over the same route, except by special permission from the Interstate Commerce Commission.

FRAME HOUSE. A house built on a wooden framework.

FRANCHISE. (1) Authorization by a government of a right or privilege to conduct certain activities (e.g., a *franchise* to operate a mass transit system). (2) Authorization given by a firm to an individual or another firm to sell or distribute the first company's products, or to operate an establishment such as a restaurant or motel.

FRANCHISE TAX. A tax levied by a governmental body on a company for the privilege of operating within an area.

FREE ENTERPRISE. An economic system based upon private ownership and operation of business with little or no government control.

FREEHOLD. (1) Tenure of an estate or office for life. (2) An estate in fee simple for life.

FREE ON BOARD (FOB). Goods delivered to the buyer at the point of manufacture and the buyer pays all freight charges from that point.

FREE PORT. (1) A port open to all trading vessels on equal terms. (2) The whole or part of a port area where no customs or duties are levied on foreign goods intended for transhipment rather than as import (not necessarily served by water; see *port*).

FREE TRADE. International commerce free from government regulations and from import or export duties.

FREEWAY. A high-speed highway free of tolls. Usually skirting areas of high population and devoid of grade crossings.

FREIGHT BILL. Document giving description of weight, charges, taxes of a freight shipment; a waybill.

FREIGHTER. A ship used primarily for transporting cargo rather than passengers although limited accommodations for such may be available.

FREIGHT FORWARDER. A regulated common carrier that assembles and consolidates small shipments into full car or truck loads which are then moved to break-bulk stations where the small shipments are distributed to numerous destinations. Forwarder rates are similar to less-than-truckload rates and the profit must be extracted from the spread between car-truck load and less than truckload levels, less the costs of consolidation and distribution.

FRENCH DRAIN. (1) A rock drain. (2) Passages for water through loosely packed stone in a trench.

FRENCH WINDOW. A casement window with adjoining sashes attached to opposite jambs and opening in the middle.

FREQUENCY. (1) The number of cycles through which an alternating current passes per second. (2) United States frequency: 60 cycles.

FRIABLE. Fragile; easily crumbled or polverized.

FRIEZE. (1) The horizontal strip running between a cornice and an architrave. (2) Any decorative horizontal strip as along the top of the wall of a room.

FRINGE AREA. The portion of a municipality immediately outside the central business district in which there is a wide range in type of business activity, including some industrial, etc.

FRINGE BENEFITS. The benefits accruing to a worker beyond his normal wages such as vacation, insurance, etc.

FROG. A track structure used at the intersection of two running rails to provide support for railroad car wheels and passageways for their flanges, thus permitting the wheels on either rail to cross the other.

FRONTAGE. (1) The front part of a building or a lot. (2) Land adjacent to a street, highway, or railroad. (3) Land lying between the front of a building and the street.

FRONTAGE ROAD. (1) A road contiguous to and generally parallel to a main highway and designed to permit access to the main road from a subdivision. (2) A service road.

FRONT FOOT. (1) A foot of land measured along the frontage of a lot. (2) "Sales price per *front foot*" usually is the basis of sale of urban commercial property and includes the ground lying back of the frontages to the rear boundary of the property.

FROST BOX. A box surrounding pipes to prevent freezing.

FRUITER. A ship that carries fruit (e.g., a banana boat).

FUEL COSTS. As commonly used by the electric utility companies, costs are usually computed in cents per million BTUs consumed; i.e., the total cost of fuel consumed divided by its total BTU content, the answer thus resulting is then multiplied by one million.

FULCRUM. The support on which a lever rests or about which it turns when raising a weight.

FULL TRAILER. A truck trailer with wheels at both ends, unlike the semi-trailer which has wheels only at the rear and rests on the fifth wheel of the tractor.

FUNDED DEBT. The long-term debt which has arisen from the sale or assumption of debt securities with maturities of more than one year.

FUSEE. A red flare used for warning and flagging purposes.

FUSIBLE. Capable of being fused or melted by heat.

FUSION. The formation of a heavier nucleus from two lighter ones with the attendant release of nuclear energy.

G

GABLE. The outside, triangular section of a wall extending upward from the level of the eaves of an uncurved, sloped roof to the ridge pole.

GABLE ROOF. A roof that forms a gable.

GAGE, GAUGE. The distance between gage lines measured at right angles thereto. (Standard railroad *gage* is 4'8½''.)

GALVANOMETER. An apparatus for indicating the pressure and determining the strength and direction of an electric current.

GALVANOSCOPE. An instrument for detecting electric current and indicating its direction.

GAMBREL ROOF. A ridged roof with the slope broken on each side so that the lower section has the steeper pitch.

GANDY DANCER. A slang expression for a railroad-track worker.

GANGUE. The worthless minerals found in a vein of ore.

GANTRY. A bridge-like framework for holding the rails for a traveling crane or for supporting railroad signals.

GARNISHEE. To attach personal income to pay a legal debt.

GARNISHMENT. Attachment of wages to pay a debt. Not permitted in a number of states nor by the federal government.

GATE MONEY. The total amount of income from admissions to an event prior to payment of expenses; the gross.

GATEWAY. A point where freight moving from one territory to another is interchanged between transportation lines, such as at Chicago and St. Louis.

GENERAL WARRANTY. A covenant in a deed whereby the grantor agrees to protect the grantee against the world.

GEODESIC DOME. A light, but strongly built hemispherical dome made of prefabricated polyhedral lattice modules and covered with a thin but strong material.

GEODYNAMICS, The branch of geography concerned with the forces affecting the structure of the earth.

GEOGRAPHICAL MILE. 6,080.2 feet; one-sixtieth of a degree of the earth's equator.

GERRYMANDER. To alter the boundaries of a voting district so as to advance unfairly the interests of a political faction or party.

GHETTO. A slum area or run-down section of a city usually inhabited by the poor and minority groups.

GIB. A plate machined to hold other parts in place to afford a bearing surface or to provide means for taking up wear.

GIRDER. A lone, heavy beam of wood or metal acting as a main horizontal support for the framework of a structure.

GLACIS. A slope—especially a defensive slope around a fortification.

GLOST. (1) Glazed pottery. (2) Lead used in making pottery.

GNEISS. A coarse-grained rock consisting of the same components as granite, containing feldspar.

GONDOLA. (1) A large, flat-bottomed river boat or scow. (2) A railroad flat car with sides and open top.

GOOD WILL. An intangible asset of a company in terms of prestige, good name, and reputation for good relations with customers.

GRABEN. A depression of land caused by the downward faulting of a portion of the earth's crust.

GRADE. (1) The ratio of rise or fall of the grade line to its length. (2) To prepare ground by leveling.

GRADE CROSSING. An intersection of rights of way at a common level.

GRADE LINE. The line on a profile representing the tops of the embankments and the bottoms of the cuts.

GRADE SCHOOL. An elementary school consisting of the first six or eight grades. (In some areas Junior High School starts at grade seven or eight.)

GRADE SEPARATION. A structure built to vertically separate two or more intersecting roadways.

GRADIENT. (1) Degree of incline in a slope. (2) A ramp. (3) The rate of inclination of the grade line from the horizontal.

GRANDFATHER CLAUSE. An exemption by which those who have been operating prior to a certain date are not affected by an enactment of a regulation, law, or proceeding.

GRAND JURY. A body of persons, not fewer than twelve nor more than twenty-four, called to hear complaints and to determine whether there is sufficient evidence to warrant indictment.

GRANGE. The Order of the Patrons of Husbandry, an association of United States farmers founded in 1867 to promote agricultural interests.

GRANIFORM. A term used to describe hard-grained igneous rock.

GRANT-IN-AID. A grant of funds by a government or private group to a local agency for assistance.

GRAPNEL. A small anchor with several flukes at the end of the shank to seize or hold objects; a grappling iron or hook.

GRATIS. Free.

GRATUITOUS. Given or obtained without requirement of payment.

GREAT GROSS. A dozen dozen dozen =1,728.

GRESHAM'S LAW. The principal stating that of two forms of currency of equal face value but of unequal exchange, the less valuable tends to drive the other from circulation owing to the hoarding of the preferred form.

GRID. An arrangement of regularly-spaced parallel or intersecting bars, wires, etc.

GRID BIAS. Voltage applied to the grid of an electron tube to make it negative with respect to the cathode.

GRID LEAK. A resistor connected between the grid and cathode of an electron tube to allow the escape of excessive negative charges from the grid.

GRILLE. A grating used as a divider, barrier, screen, trap, etc.

GRISTMILL. A factory for grinding grain; a flour mill.

GROIN. A barrier extending into the water from a beach to arrest traveling sand and give protection against wave-wash.

GROSS LEASE. A rental or lease or property whereby the lessor is to meet all property charges regularly incurred through ownership.

GROSS NATIONAL PRODUCT (GNP). The total market value of a nations's goods and services before any deductions or allowances are made.

GROSS TON. A long ton; 2,240 pounds.

GROSS WEIGHT. (1) The weight of the article together with its container and packing material. (2) The total weight of contents and the railroad car or motor vehicle hauling the contents.

GROTTO. A cave, or cave-like structure.

GROUND RENT. Payment for the rights to build on, make improvements on, or occupy, a piece of land.

GROUNDWATER. Water beneath the earth's surface; the supply of such by means of wells.

GROUND WAVE. A radio wave that travels along the surface of the ground rather than in the air.

GROUND WIRE. The wire connecting an electrical device with the ground, or a grounded object, to eliminate damage or injury resulting from overload, lightning, shorting, etc.

GROUNDWORK. A foundation.

GROUT. A fluid mixture of cement, water, and sand.

GRUBBING. Removal of stumps and roots from a tract.

GUANO. (1) Fertilizer. (2) The accumulated excrement of sea birds.

GUARANTEE. (1) A pledge; warranty. (2) One who receives a guaranty.

GUARANTOR. One who grants or gives a warranty or guaranty.

GUARANTY. A pledge or promise to fulfill a contract, debt, or duty of another in case of default or miscarriage by that person.

GUARDIAN. One who is legally assigned care of a person or property.

GUESTIMATE. An estimate based on nothing more than guesswork.

GUILLOCHE. An ornamental pattern or border composed of two or more curved bands or lines which intertwine.

GULCH. A deep, narrow ravine cut out by a rushing stream, spring, or flash flood.

GULF STATES. Alabama, Florida, Louisiana, Mississippi, Texas.

GULLY. A ravine cut out by running water.

GUM ARABIC. The gum from various species of acacia used in ink, candy, medicine, etc.

GUNWALE. The upper edge of the sides of a boat.

GUSHER. An oil well that spurts oil without need of pumps.

GUTTA PERCHA. A grayish-white rubber formed from the juices and saps of various Maylayan trees.

GYROMAGNETIC. Of or pertaining to any relationship between the magnetic properties of a body and its rotational motion.

H

HABENDUM CLAUSE. The covenant which defines the quantity of the estate granted in the deed.

HACIENDA. (1) A landed estate. (2) A farming, mining, or manufacturing establishment in a rural area, particularly in southwestern United States and Mexico.

HACK. (1) A railroad caboose. (2) A taxicab. (3) A conveyance to transport passengers from a terminal to a hotel, etc.

HA-HA. A hedge or wall or sunken fence set low in the ground so as not to obstruct the view.

HAND. Four inches.

HARBOR LINE. The line defining the limits of a port.

HARD COAL. Anthracite coal.

HARDPAN. A layer of very hard clay-like matter underlying the softer topsoil.

HARD RUBBER. Vulcanite. (Vulcanized rubber is crude rubber treated with sulfur compounds under varying degrees of heat to increase its strength and elasticity.)

HARDSTAND. A paved or hard-surfaced area for parking or outdoor storage of materials.

HARD WATER. Water containing, in solution, salts, of calcium and magesium, which inhibit soap lathering.

HARDWOODS. (1) Deciduous trees such as oak, hickory, ash or maple, as distinguished from coniferous trees. (2) One of the group of trees having broad leaves. The term *hardwood* has no reference to the actual hardness of the wood.

HAWAIIAN TECHNIQUE. A "sandwich" lease in which the owner leases to a tenant, who in turn subleases to a secondary tenant. This technique is so named because of William Zeckendorf's claim to having originated the method in Hawaii. (Also know as the "Pineapple Technique.")

HEADWATERS. The source of a stream.

HEARSAY EVIDENCE. Evidence of a declaration made out of court. Typically, testimony of a witness as to what another person told him. (Generally not admissible as legal evidence.)

HEARTWOOD. The inner core of a tree trunk comprising the "annual rings" and containing nonliving elements."

HEAT MELT. The steel resulting from one charge of the melting furnace.

HEAT PUMP. A year-round air-conditioning system employing refrigeration equipment in a manner which enables usable heat to be supplied during the winter and by reversing the operation cycle to abstract heat from the area during the summer. When operating as a heating system, heat is absorbed from air, water, or earth and this heat together with the heat equivalent of the work of compression is supplied to the area to be heated. When operating on the cooling cycle, heat is absorbed from the area to be cooled and this heat together with the heat equivalent of the work of compression is rejected to the outside medium.

HEIR APPARENT. One who must, by course of law, become the heir if he survives his ancestor.

HEIR PRESUMPTIVE. An heir whose claim to an estate may become void by the birth of a nearer relative.

HELIPORT. A landing area for helicopters and autogiros.

HEREDITAMENTS. The largest classification of real property; includes land, buildings, rights-of-way, easements, etc.

HERTZ. A unit of electromagnetic wave frequency equal to one cycle per second.

HETERODOX. At variance with accepted and established doctrines.

HEXAGON. A six-sided polygon.

HIGH SCHOOL. Education following elementary school, typically comprising grades nine through twelve.

HIGHWAY. Any road or thoroughfare, but especially a main road of some length that is open to the public; a freeway.

HINTERLAND. (1) An inland region immediately adjacent to a coastal area. (2) A remote region away from urban areas; back country.

HIPPODROME. An arena, usually enclosed, utilized for horse shows, circuses, and other large and extensive productions.

HISTORICAL COST. Capital cost rates at the time the securities were actually sold, applicable for long-term debt and preferred stock.

HOBSON'S CHOICE. A choice in which one must take what is offered or nothing. (Derived from Thomas Hobson, an English liveryman who required each customer to take the horse nearest the barn door.)

HOGSHEAD. (1) A large cask. (2) A liquid measure generally agreed to be 63 gallons, or 8.42 cubic feet.

HOLDING COMPANY. A company which invests in the stocks of one or more companies which it may then control.

HOMESTEAD ACT. An 1862 act of Congress providing settlers with 160 acres of free public lands for cultivation and improvement and eventual ownership after meeting certain requirements.

HOMESTEAD LAW. A law in many states exempting up to a certain amount of a dwelling and land from certain tax liabilities. (Florida, for example, exempts $5,000 of value of owner-occupied dwelling from assessment for property taxes.)

HONOR. To accept and pay a note, draft, or bill.

HONORARIUM. Payment made to a professional person for services rendered when law or custom forbids a set fee (e.g., payment made to a professional for presenting a paper at a formal meeting).

HOPPER. Any of various funnel-shaped receptacles in which loose materials (grain, coal, sand, etc.) may be stored until ready for discharge through the bottom into a transportation vehicle.

HOPPER CAR. A railroad freight car open at the top and with sides extending upward from the bed. The bottom of the car may be opened for speedy discharge of cargo.

HORSE LATITUDES. A belt of high pressure at about the 35° north and south latitudes characterized by calms and light variable winds.

HORSEPOWER. The standard unit of the rate of work equal to 550 pounds lifted one foot in one second; or 33,000 pounds one foot in one minute.

HOTBOX. An overheated journal of a railroad car caused by excessive friction between the bearing and the journal, lack of lubricant, or foreign and abrasive material.

HOUSE OF DELEGATES. The lower house of the legislatures of Maryland, Virginia, and West Virginia. Most other states refer to this lower house as the House of Representatives.

HOUSEOMINIUM. A house sold and occupied under the same regulations and agreements as a condominium apartment. The occupant is the owner of the house and pays a monthly fee for maintenance in addition to regular or mortgage payments. This fee pays for yard and outside building maintenance, but does not include inside repairs or refurbishing.

HOUSE TRACK. A railroad track serving a freight depot.

HOWK. To dig.

HUMP. An incline in a railroad yard over which freight cars are uncoupled and permitted to roll free into a classification track.

HUNDRED. A subdivision of a county (still used in Delaware).

HUSBANDRY. (1) The occupation of business of farming. (2) Management of household affairs. (3) *Animal husbandry* is the breeding and raising of livestock.

HYDROSTAT. A device for preventing the explosion of a steam boiler due to the lack of water.

HYPOTHECATE. To pledge personal property or security for debt without the actual transfer of possession.

I

I-BEAM. A beam or joist that in cross-section has the shape of the letter "I."

ICING STATION. A point at which facilities are maintained for supplying ice to reefer cars and trucks for the protection of perishable freight.

IGNEOUS ROCK. Rock formed by the action of great heat within the earth.

IMMOVABLES. Real estate and appurtenances which must pass with the sale of a property.

IMPERIUM. (1) The right to command. (2) Authority to use the force of the state to enforce its laws.

IMPERMEABLE. Impervious to moisture.

IMPERVIOUS. Incapable of being passed through as by moisture or light rays.

IMPIGNORATE. To mortgage or pawn.

IMPLICIT. Implied or understood but not specifically expressed.

IMPOST. (1) To classify for purposes of determining customs duties. (2) The tax or duty imposed.

IMPOUND. (1) To collect water in a pond, reservoir, etc. (2) To seize and place in the custody of a court.

IMPRESS. To establish a voltage in a conductor or circuit by means of a dynamo, battery, or other source of electric energy.

IMPREST. A loan or prepayment of money from public funds, as in an *imprest account.*

IMPRIMATUR. Authorization, especially official license or approval for publication of a work.

IMPROVEMENTS. Buildings, fences, etc.; useful additions to real property.

IMPUTE. Ascribe; attribute.

IN ABSENTIA. In absence.

INALIENABLE. Not transferable; cannot be rightfully taken.

IN BOND SHIPMENT. An import or export shipment which has not been cleared through customs.

INCHOATE. Incipient; barely begun; lacking order, form or coherence.

INCOME, EARNED. Income from labor, business transactions, or other activities in which personal effort of the recipient is involved.

INCOME, UNEARNED. Income received from rent, interest, dividends, etc.

INCONVERTIBLE. Incapable of being changsd, exchanged, or converted —especially paper money not exchangeable for scrip or other specie.

INCORPORATE. To form a legally recognized corporation.

INCREMENT. The act of increasing or growing larger.

INCREMENT, UNEARNED. Any increase of value produced by forces independent of the person who receives it (e.g., the increase in land value as a result of increased population, etc.).

INCUBATOR BUILDING. Multitenancy by small businesses in a single building.

INDEMNIFY. (1) To compensate for loss or damage. (2) To insure. (3) To give security against future loss.

INDEMNITEE. One who is indemnified.

INDEMNITOR. One who indemnifies.

INDEMNITY. That which is paid for loss or damage.

INDENTURE. A deed or other contract between two or more parties.

INDETERMINATE. Not definite in extent or nature.

INDIRECT TAX. A tax, such as a customs duty, the burden of which is ultimately passed on to another as in the form of higher prices.

INDICT. To charge with a crime; accuse.

INDITE. To write.

INDUCTION COIL. A device consisting of two concentric coils and an interrupter that changes a low steady voltage into high intermittent voltage by magnetic induction.

INDUSTRIAL COLONY. (1) A tract of land occupied by a number of industries not neccessarily under restrictive covenants. (2) A building, or series of buildings, usually interconnected and occupied by a number of different firms.

INDUSTRIAL DEVELOPMENT AUTHORITY. The financial arm of a state or other political subdivision established for the purpose of financing economic development in an area, usually through loans to non-profit organizations, which in turn provide facilities for manufacturing and other industrial operations.

INDUSTRIAL DISTRICT. A subdivided tract of land, suitably located with respect to utilities and transportation facilities which is restricted and promoted solely for industrial purposes by a sponsoring managerial group with the express purpose of protecting the investment of both the developers and the occupants of the *district*.

INDUSTRIAL MIX AND SHIFT ANALYSIS. An analysis to determine the "standing" of manufacturing operations in a particular area versus the nation as a whole. (This is explained in more detail in the Handbook section of this book.)

INDUSTRIAL PARK. A *planned industrial park* is a special and exclusive type of industrial subdivision prepared according to a comprehensive plan to provide serviced sites for a community of compatible industrial operations. The park, under continuing management, provides for the absolute control of the tract and buildings through restrictive covenants and/or adequate zoning, with a view toward maintaining aesthetic value and protecting the environment throughout the development.

INDUSTRIAL PROPERTY MORTGAGE. The mortgage covers not only real estate but also fixtures and equipment and even those fixtures and equipment added subsequent to the date of execution of the mortgage.

INDUSTRIAL RAILROAD. A short railroad owned or controlled by one or more of the principal industries served by it.

INDUSTRIAL REALTOR. A person engaged in the industrial real estate business who is a member of the Society of Industrial Realtors and the National Association of Real Estate Boards.

INDUSTRIAL RELATIONS. Relations between management and workers with respect to working conditions.

INDUSTRIAL SITE. A tract of land suitable for an industrial building which is within the economic reach of transportation, utilities, and so controlled by ownership in fee simple that it can be offered at a firm price to a buyer.

INDUSTRIAL TRACK. A railroad spur track serving one or more industries.

INDUSTRIAL TRACT. A land area reserved for industrial development, through ownership, zoning, or both.

INDUSTRY. Any specific branch of production or manufacture. Also may include distribution and other services. Present day nomenclature speaks of recreation as being an industry and even retail and wholesale trade may be included in the category labeled "industry." However, strictly speaking, manufacturing operations are usually referred to as industrial operations.

INFEUDATION. The granting of an estate in fee.

INFLAMMABLE. Materials, usually liquid, that give off vapors which become combustible at certain temperatures are *inflammables*.

INFLUENT. That which flows in as a tributary into a larger stream.

INFRASTRUCTURE. Originally, the military installations supported by NATO; the term has now come to mean the basic framework and facilities or substructure of a community or area.

INGOT. A mass of cast metal from a crucible or mold.

INGOT IRON. Extremely pure iron, rust-resistant and widely used as a construction material.

INHERENT ADVANTAGE. A natural benefit. The Interstate Commerce Commission by law is required to recognize and preserve the *inherent advantages* of each mode of transportation.

INJUNCTION. A judicial order requiring the party enjoined to take or refrain from taking some specific action.

INLIER. An outcrop of older rock surrounded by later strata.

IN LIEU OF. (1) Instead of. (2) A substitute.

IN LOCO. In place; in the right spot.

IN LOCO PARENTIS. In place of a parent; a guardian.

IN-PLACE DENSITY. The normal resistance to compression and compaction by soil which is in its natural location and consistency.

INPUT. (1) Energy or labor put into a product or work. (2) Information fed into a computer.

IN RE. As to; concerning.

IN REM. The thing; not directed against any specific person or group of people.

IN SITU. In its original site or position.

INSOLATE. Expose to the rays of the sun as for bleaching, drying, etc.

INSOLVENCY. Bankruptcy.

INSPISSATE. To thicken by evaporation.

INSTALLMENT CONTRACT. Purchase of real estate on an installment basis in which, upon default of any payment, all prior payments are forfeited.

INSTANT. The current month.

IN STATU QUO. In the present, or original, condition.

INSULATION. (1) The material installed between walls, ceiling, pipes, etc., to prevent leakage of heat, sound, radiation, etc. (2) A material wrapped or formed around wires to protect from electric shock or leakage of power.

INSURABLE INTEREST. Such interest as will legally permit a person to obtain interest in the life or property of another.

INTANGIBLE. Lacking physical substance.

INTEGRAL. (1) Constituent. (2) Essential part of the whole.

INTER ALIA. Among other things.

INTER ALIOS. Among other persons.

INTERCEPTION DITCH. An open artificial waterway for diverting surface water from its natural course of flow.

INTERCEPTOR SEWER. A sewer main diverting sewage from one main to another or to another course.

INTERCHANGE. (1) A system of interconnecting roadways in conjunction with one or more grade separations providing for the interchange of traffic between two or more roadways on different levels. (2) A point, community, or other location of interchange of traffic between two or more railroads.

INTERCHANGE TRACK. A railroad track on which cars are delivered or received between two or more railroads.

INTERCOMMUNITY. The condition of being common to two or more; mutuality.

INTERCOURSE. Mutual exchange of commerce or communications.

INTERDICT. To debar or prohibit.

INTEREST. (1) The cost of borrowing money, over and above the principal. (2) Proportionate ownership of a party in a property held in partnership with others.

INTERFACE. Literally, a surface forming the common boundary between adjacent spaces.

INTERLINE. Interchange between two railroad companies. (Said of freight moving over the lines of two or more transportation companies in order to reach a destination.)

INTERLINE WAYBILL. A waybill covering the movement of freight over the lines of two or more railroads.

INTERMITTENT WATER TREATING PLANT. A plant so designed that the water is pumped alternately to two or more treating tanks, where chemicals are added, and there retained until chemical reactions and precipitation are completed.

INTERMODEL DISTRIBUTION CENTER. A facility served by more than one mode of transportation (e.g., A rail-truck terminal).

INTERNAL COMBUSTION ENGINE. A prime mover in which energy is released from the rapid-burning of a fuel-air mixture and is thus converted into mechanical energy.

INTERNATIONAL CANDLE. A unit of luminous intensity defined as *standard* from 1921 to 1940 and since discarded as a measurement of light. Formerly the light emitted by five square millimeters of platinum at the temperature of solidification.

INTERNATIONAL NAUTICAL MILE. A distance by sea of 1,852 meters or 6,076.105 feet.

INTERPLEADER. A proceeding in which one who has money or goods claimed by two or more persons may ask that the claimants be required to litigate the title among and between themselves.

INTERPOLATE. (1) To insert; make additions. (2) To introduce additions into a discourse. (3) To insert unacknowledged additions in order to falsify a text. (4) To insert intermediate terms in, as a series according to the law of the series.

INTER SE. Between themselves.

INTERSECTION LEG. That part of any one of the roadways radiating from an intersection which is outside the area of the intersection proper; the approach or exit to or from an intersection.

INTERSTATE. Between, among, or involving different states.

INTERSTATE COMMERCE COMMISSION (ICC). A federal regulatory body for overseeing operations in interstate commerce.

INTESTATE. Without a will.

INTRADOS. The inner, or concave, surface of an arch.

INTRAMUROS. Within the walls.

INTRANSIGENT. Refusing to compromise or come to terms.

INTRASTATE. Confined within or pertaining to a single state.

INTUMESCE. To swell; bubble up.

INVARIANT. Not subject to change; constant.

INVENTORY FINANCING. Borrowing or lending funds based on the value of an inventory of goods.

INVESTITURE. The act or ceremony of investing authority within an office as a right.

INVESTMENT BANKING. A field of business the function of which is participation in new capital financing for new and established businesses as well as governmental bodies; a bonding house.

INVESTMENT COMPANY. An organization that manages the pooled capital of its investors or stockholders. A *closed end investment company* issues a set amount of capital stock and issues no new shares at any time subsequent to the original offering. An *open end investment company* issues shares on demand and without limit.

INVESTMENT CREDIT. Credit extended to a business for purchase of real estate, equipment, or other fixed assets.

INVESTMENT TAX CREDIT. Credit against income taxes provided for in qualified depreciated assets.

INVESTMENT TRUST. An open-end investment company; a mutual fund.

INVESTOR-OWNED UTILITIES. Business in the field of utilities organized as tax-paying companies usually financed by the sale of securities in the free market.

IONIC. A type of architecture characterized by scroll-like ornaments usually at the top of a column.

IPSE DIXIT. An unproved or dogmatic expression.

IPSO FACTO. By the fact itself.

IPSO JURE. By the law itself.

IRONWOOD. Various trees having hard, heavy and strong wood (e.g., the Catalina ironwood found in Southern California).

ISOGON. A polygon having equal angles.

ITEM VETO. The power or action of a head of government to veto parts of a piece of legislation without vetoing the entire act.

ITERUM. Again; once more.

J

JACK PINE. A pine tree growing in a barren area.

JAKES. An outdoor privy; an outhouse.

JETSAM. Goods thrown into the sea to lighten an imperiled vessel.

JETTISON. (1) To discard. (2) Jetsam.

JETTY. (1) A wharf, pier. (2) A structure extending into a body of water to direct current for purposes of protecting a harbor or shoreline from erosion.

JIB. A triangular sail.

JOBBER. Wholesaler who operates on a small scale and sells only to retail establishments and institutions.

JOHNSON GRASS. A perennial grass valued for hay but considered a weed in carefully cultivated land tracts.

JOINDER. (1) A joining of causes of action or defense in a complaint. (2) A joining of partners as plaintiffs or defendants in a legal action. (3) The formal acceptance of an issue tendered.

JOINT FACILITY. Railroad property which two or more rail carriers either jointly own, maintain, or operate by formal agreement.

JOINT STOCK COMPANY. An unincorporated business association of a group of parties each of whom owns shares which he may sell or transfer at any time.

JOINT TENANCY. Property held by two or more persons together with distinct character of survivorship.

JOINTURE. A settlement of property made to a female by her husband for her use after his death.

JOIST. Any of the parallel beams placed horizontally from wall to wall to which the flooring or laths of the ceiling may be fastened.

JOULE. A unit of work equal to $0.7373+$ foot pounds.

JOURNAL BOX. The box or bearing for the rotating axle of a railroad car. The metal housing which encloses the journal of a railroad car axle.

JUDGMENT. Decree of a court declaring that an individual is indebted to others and fixing the amount of such indebtedness.

JUDICATORY. Pertaining to the administration of justice.

JUMPER. A wire used to cut out part of a circuit, or to close a temporary gap in it.

JUNIOR COLLEGE. An institution offering college courses through the sophomore year of college.

JUNIOR HIGH SCHOOL. A school intermediate between elementary and high school—typically grades 7 and 8, and sometimes 9.

JUNIOR MORTGAGE. (1) A second mortgage. (2) A mortgage subordinate to a previous one.

JUNTA. A body of people gathered together for some secret purpose; a cabal.

JURAL. Pertaining to law.

JURAT. The statement at the end of an affidavit listing the names of persons swearing to it and where, when, and before whom it was sworn.

JURISDICATION. (1) Authority. (2) Territory over which such authority reigns.

JURISPRUDENCED. The philosophy of law and its administration.

JUS CIVILE. Civil law.

JUS GENTIUM. The law of nations.

JUTTY. Jetty.

K

KAIN, KANE. (1) Barter. (2) Rental or tax paid in produce or livestock.

KAOLIN. A hydrous aluminum silicate used in making procelain.

KAURI GUM. A resin exuded by the New Zealand *kauri* tree used in linoleum varnishes and the like.

KECKLE. To wrap as a protection against chafing, (as a cable with rope, canvas, etc.).

KEDGE. A light anchor used in freeing a vessel from a reef, etc.

KEEL. The main structural member of a vessel running fore to aft along the bottom of the boat.

KEELSON. A beam running above the keel to lend added strength to the vessel.

KEG. A small barrel holding from five to ten gallons of liquid or 100 pounds of nails.

KENCH. A bin for salting fish.

KERF. (1) The cut or notch made by a saw, axe, etc. (2) The amount or piece cut off.

KEY INDUSTRY. (1) The important industry to an area. (2) The industry which may, because of its needs or services, induce other industries to locate in proximity to it.

KEY-IN-THE-LOCK. A "package" plant whereby an industry may be provided with land, building, and equipment with rental/lease covering all aspects. This type of deal is often offered by local development corporations in order to induce a firm to locate in a specific area. Builders with sound financial backing may also contract to provide the complete "package" so as to allow the client to retain his working capital for use in operations of the plant.

KEYSTONE. The uppermost and last-set stone in an arch.

KICKBACK. (1) Graft. (2) Extra-legal commission paid for certain services rendered in procuring business or other favors.

KIER. A vat in which fabrics are boiled and bleached.

KILN. An oven for baking, drying, or burning, bricks, lime, lumber, pottery etc.

KILN DRY. To dry in a kiln.

KILO. Kilogram; 1,000 grams.

KILOCALORIE. The amount of heat required to raise the temperature of one Kilogram of water one degree centigrade.

KILOCYCLE. 1,000 cycles per second.

KILOGRAM. 1,000 grams.

KILOVOLT. 1,000 volts.

KILOVOLT-AMPERE (KVA). 1,000 volt amperes.

KILOWATT. 1,000 watts.

KILOWATT HOUR. The work done, or the energy resulting from one kilowatt acting for one hour; equal to 1.34 horsepower hours.

KINETIC. Pertaining to motion.

KNAR. A knot on a tree or in wood.

KNOCKED-DOWN (KD). (1) An article taken apart for ease of shipment. (2) Unassembled merchandise or freight.

KNOT. One nautical mile per hour (6,076.12 feet) equivalent to 1.15078 land miles per hour.

KNOW-HOW. Expertise; knowledge concerning particular subjects.

KNURL. A lump or protuberance as along a metal object.

L

LABORATORY SCHOOL. A school for educational experimentation.

LABOR MARKET AREA. The area within which workers will travel to work.

LABOR RELATIONS. (1) Industrial relations. (2) Relations between management and employes.

LABOR TURNOVER. The change in a company's labor force caused by quits, discharges, layoffs, retirements, replacements, etc.

LACHES. Unreasonable delay or negligence in asserting one's rights.

LACUNA. (1) A small pit, hollow, or depression. (2) A gap in an argument or written work.

LACUSTRINE. Of or relating to, or growing in, a lake.

LADDER TRACK. The main track of a railroad yard from which individual tracks lead off; also called "lead track."

LAGGING. Strips of sheeting used to transfer weight or pressure to centering or other supporting members. Commonly used in the construction of tunnels, arches and shafts.

LAGOON. A body of shallow water.

LAITANCE. A film of scum consisting of very fine particles which separate from freshly deposited mortar or concrete.

LAME DUCK. An officeholder whose term continues beyond the election of a successor to his office.

LANCET ARCH. A narrow, acutely-pointed arch.

LANCET WINDOW. A narrow, acutely-pointed window.

LAND BANK. (1) A bank which makes loans on real property. (2) A reserve of land "banked" for specific purposes.

LAND CONTRACT. A contract for the purchases of real estate on an installment basis. Deed to the property is passed to the purchaser after the last payment is received by the seller.

LAND GRANT. Government land given for a specific purpose, as to a railroad or university.

LANDLOCKED. A property surrounded by other ownerships to which there is no road access. (Easement must be obtained for right of access.)

LANDLORD. The owner of property leased to another.

LAND OFFICE. A government office for the transaction of business pertaining to public lands.

LAND-POOR. Ownership of such large tracts of land (or numbers of tracts) that yields do not cover expenses.

LAND USE. Occupancy of lands for certain uses as: (1) *Central Business District* (CBD): the downtown business section of a city. (2) *Fringe area:* the portion of a community immediately outside the CBD and usually consisting of small business, services and some mixed residential uses. (3) *Outlying Business District:* An area some distance from

70

the CBD and its fringe area such as a neighborhood or regional shopping center. (4) *Residential.* (5) *Industrial Area:* industrial districts and individual factories, warehouses and service centers. (6) *Recreational Areas.* (7) *Public Buildings:* government officers; fire and police facilities, etc. (8) *Agricultural:* including farming, dairying and raising of livestock.

LAND USE MAP. A multicolored map indicating various uses of land in an area. (Not to be confused with the *zoning map*.)

LANE. A narrow road or walkway.

LAP JOINT. A joint wherein a layer of material *laps* over another.

LARBOARD. The left side of a boat as one faces forward; port.

LARGESS. Liberal giving; also something being given.

LATESCENT. Obscure; latent.

LATH. A thin strip of wood or metal.

LATHE. A machine that turns materials so that they may be shaped.

LATITUDE. Distance north and south of the equator measured in degrees.

LAVATORY. Washroom.

LEACH. To filter or cause liquid to percolate through a material.

LEAD TRACK. An extended railroad track connecting either end of a railroad yard with the main track; a ladder track.

LEAGUE. Approximately three miles. (Varies from 2.42 to 4.6 miles in various countries.)

LEASE. A rental contract.

LEASEBACK. A transaction whereby the buyer of real property leases it back to the seller thus providing working capital for the seller.

LEASEHOLD. Tenure by lease.

LEASE-PURCHASE. A transaction whereby a lessee may at some time purchase the property he is occupying under lease. Some such arrangements allow rental payments to apply toward the purchase price.

LEEWARD. (1) The direction toward which the wind is blowing. (2) Being on or toward the side sheltered from the wind.

LEGAL RESERVES. The amount of money kept available by a bank to meet the demands of depositors as specified by law in the form of a percentage of its total deposits.

LEGAL TENDER. Coin or other money which may be legally offered in payment of a debt, which must be accepted by the creditor.

LEGATEE. One to whom a legacy has been bequeathed.

LEGATOR. One who makes a will; a testator.

LEHR. A long oven in which glass is annealed.

LESE MAJESTY. (1) Treason. (2) An offense against a sovereign authority.

LESS CARLOAD (LCL). A quantity of freight less than the amount required to obtain a carload rate which, because of large quantity, is carried at a lower freight charge than less carload.

LESSEE. One to whom a lease is granted; a tenant.

LESSOR. A landlord; one who grants a lease.

LESS THAN TRUCKLOAD (LTL). A quantity of freight weighing less than that required for application of truckload rates, which, because of quantity, is carried at a lower freight charge than less than truckload.

LETTER OF ADVICE. In commerce, the letter setting forth information from a shipper to a consignee.

LETTER OF CREDIT. A statement issued to a financial institution authorizing the bearer to draw money from the institution or its branches.

LETTERS PATENT. The instrument granting a patent by a government.

LEVEE. An embankment; a flood wall.

LEVEL CROSSING. A railroad or highway intersection at grade.

LEVEL OF SERVICE. A term denoting various operating conditions.

LEVEL TERRAIN. (1) Any combination of gradients, length of grade, etc., that permits trucks to maintain speeds that equal or approach the speed of passenger cars. (2) A building site lacking either borrow or fill material, which may or may not be a detriment to the building's location. (Disadvantages may include lack of sufficient grade for water run-off of storm sewers, etc.)

LEVY. Tax; fine; assessment, etc.

LEVY EN MASSE. A spontaneous arming for defense by civilians in time of military emergency.

LEX LOCI. Local law; the law of the place.

LEX SCRIPTI. Statute law.

LIABILITY. That for which one is responsible.

LIBEL. Written or graphic representation that damages a person's reputation.

LIBELANT. One who institutes a lawsuit under the laws of libel.

LIBELEE. The defendant in a suit of libel.

LICENSE. (1) Permission or privilege. (2) A document permitting a specific activity.

LICENSEE. One to whom a license is issued.

LICENSOR. One who issues a license.

LICH-GATE. A roofed gateway to a churchyard or cemetery.

LIEN. (1) A legal right to claim or dispose of property in payment of a debt. (2) A hold or claim which one party has upon the property of another as security for some debt or claim.

LIFE ESTATE. An estate or interest held during the term of one's life.

LIGHTER. A barge or scow-like vessel used for transporting goods from dockside (or railroad) to a ship for loading and returning goods from a vessel to dockside. May also be utilized to transport shipments from one dockside to another across a harbor.

LIGHTERAGE. (1) The conveying of cargo by lighter. (2) The charges made for such services.

LIGNITE. A "coal" intermediate between peat and bituminous coal of a wood origin.

LIMITATION. (1) A restrictive condition or stipulation. (2) A legally fixed period within which certain acts may be performed if they are to be valid.

LIMITED ACCESS HIGHWAY. A main roadway prohibiting access except at certain legally defined points.

LIMITED COMPANY PARTNERSHIP. A corporation restricted in liability to the amount invested by shareholders in its stock.

LINE HAUL. (1) Transportation of cargo over one railroad. (2) That portion of the transportation service performed by one carrier.

LINE OF CREDIT. Credit extended by a financial institution to a firm in a certain amount which may be drawn on by the firm as needed.

LINN. (1) A deep ravine. (2) A waterfall.

LINTEL. A horizontal member spanning an opening to carry a superstructure, such as over a door or window.

LINTERS. The short fibers adhering to cotton seeds after ginning.

LIQUATE. To heat a metal to melting point for separation from impurities with higher melting points.

LIQUIDATE. (1) To pay off indebtedness. (2) To distribute the assets of a company of corporation.

LIS PENDENS. The doctrine giving a court control over the property involved in a suit until judgment is rendered.

LISTEL. A narrow molding.

LISTING. (1) A description of real property (see Handbook section). (2) An *exclusive listing* is real property under contract to one realtor for sale (or lease), wherein that realtor will be entitled to a commission even if the property is sold by another.

LIST PRICE. The price of merchandise as published. Discounts, if any, are made from the list price.

LITHOLOGY. The science dealing with rock composition and structure.

LITHOSPHERE. The solid crust of the earth.

LITTORAL. Belonging to the shore of a sea or lake. Corresponds to riparian rights along a stream.

LIVE LOAD. Temporary and extraneous loads of any nature which may come upon a permanent structure (e.g., traffic moving over a bridge).

LIVE STEAM. Steam supplied directly from a boiler with full power to do work; (as distinguished from *exhaust steam*).

LLANO. A flat, treeless plain.

LOAD. (1) The amount of electric power delivered or required at any specified point on a system. (2) Demand.

LOAD DISPLACEMENT. The displacement of a vessel loaded to capacity.

LOAD FACTOR. (1) The ratio of the average load in kilowatts supplied during a designated period to the peak load in kilowatts during the same period. (2) The *load factor* in percentage may be derived by multiplying the kilowatt hours in the period by 100 and dividing by the product of the maximum demand in kilowatts and the number of hours in the period.

LOADING BAYS. The area reserved for loading and unloading railroad cars, trucks, and drays at the shipping and receiving area of a commercial or manufacturing building. Although specific needs differ, it is usually recommended that loading bays should be at least 12 feet wide with overhead clearance of 14 feet. At truck bays, the recommended length should be at least 45 feet. Local and state regulations should be checked for requirements at specific locations.

LOADING COIL. An inductance coil in a circuit to increase its period of oscillation.

LOAM. Loose-textured soil.

LOAN. Money or property provided for temporary use.

LOAN COMMITMENT. An agreement to make a loan.

LOBLOLLY. A mudhole; ooze; mire; muck.

LOBBY. (1) An entryway or vestibule; foyer. (2) A waiting room. (3) A group with common interests endeavoring to influence legislators or regulatory agencies.

LOCAL DEVLOPMENT COMPANY. An organization comprised of local citizens formed for the express purpose of improving the local economy through private financing of industrial and business projects. Under SBA, such may obtain loans up to $350,000 providing that 10 percent or more is obtained from local sources.

LOCAL DEVELOPMENT CORPORATION. An organization usually made up of local citizens of a community designed to improve the economy of the area by inducing business and industry to locate therein and expand in the area. The LDC usually has financing capabilities.

LOCAL DEVELOPMENT DISTRICT. Originally created by the Appalachian Regional Commission, a states-federal agency designed to improve the economy of a thirteen-state area extending from southern New York state to northeastern Mississippi. The LDD is a multicounty body with common interests directing its efforts toward promoting the economy and improving the way of life of the area. The LDD membership includes various representatives of the area, but must have at least 51 percent representation of local governments of the governing board of the district. The board, in turn, appoints the executive staff of the LDD, the director of which must be approved as to qualifications and capabilities by the central state government and the Appalachian Regional Commission at Washington.

LOCAL OPTION. The right of a political subdivision to restrict or allow certain activities.

LOCAL RATE. A railroad freight rate applying between stations located on single railroad company.

LOCAL REFERENDUM. A vote taken in a political subdivision to determine a course of action.

LOCATION. (1) Site. (2) A tract of land. (3) A community.

LOCKOUT. The closing of an establishment by an employer to force employes to agree to terms set by that employer.

LOCUS. Area; place; locality.

LODE. A deposit of metallic ore.

LODGE. (1) A dwelling; cabin. (2) An inn, particularly at a park.

LOFT. A large open workroom in an upper story of a building, which may be utilized for production or storage.

LOGARITHM. The power to which a fixed number must be raised to produce a given number. The "fixed number" is referred to as "the base."

LOGBOOK. The book in which official records of a ship or aircraft are kept.

LOGROLLING. The trading of influence between legislators whereby one legislator will vote for a fellow legislator's bill in return for receiving a vote for *his* pet project.

LONGITUDE. Distance east and west from *zero longitude,* which runs through Greenwich, England, measured in degrees.

LONG-TERM CAPITAL GAIN. A capital gain realized over a period of time exceeding six months.

LONG-TERM DEBT. Outstanding mortgage bonds, debentures, and notes which are due one year or more from the date of issuance.

LONG-TERM LIABILITY. (1) Long-term debt. (2) Debts payable in a time period longer than one year.

LONG TON. A gross ton; 2,240 pounds.

LOWRY PROCESS. The method of treating wood by injecting an amount of creosote in excess of final retention, the excess being removed by fast, high vacuum.

LUNT. (1) A whiff of smoke. (2) A slow-burning torch.

LUSTRUM. A period of five years.

M

MACADAM. Broken stone used in paving a road. (Named for John L. MacAdam, a Scots engineer, 1758-1836.)

MACROCOSM. (1) The whole universe. (2) A large system regarded as a unit.

MAIN. A large pipe used for transportation of water; sewage; petroleum products; gas, etc.

MAIN LINE. The principal line of a railroad company.

MAINTENANCE EXPENSES. A subdivision of operating expenses including: labor; material; and other direct and indirect costs incurred for maintaining plant and equipment.

MAIN TRACK. Railroad track extending through yards and between stations upon which trains are operated by timetable or train order or both, or the use of which is governed by signals.

MALA FIDE. In bad faith; fraudulent.

MALFEASANCE. The performance of an act that is harmful or wrong.

MALL. A promenade or walkway, usually public, shaded, and covered.

MALLEABLE. Capable of being hammered or rolled without breaking; flexible; pliable.

MALLEABLE IRON. Cast iron made tough by gradual heating and slow cooling.

MALPRACTICE. Improper or immoral conduct in a public position of trust.

MANAGED CURRENCY. A monetary system in which the amount in circulation is regulated in an attempt to control credit, prices, etc.

MANDAMUS. A writ issued by a court that something be done (e.g., a *mandamus* directed to a government to improve its sewerage).

MANDATE. Any authoritative command or charge.

MAN-HOUR. The amount of work performed by one person in one hour.

MAN-HOURS. The number of persons working multiplied by the number of hours worked.

MAN-HOURS LOST. Number of men × hours idle = *manhours lost* to productivity because of strike, slow-down, lock-out, etc.

MANIFEST. Contents of a truck or railroad car or vessel.

MANIFESTO. A public and formal declaration of principles.

MANIFEST TRAIN. A scheduled freight train.

MANOR. (1) A mansion; *manor house*. (2) A landed estate.

MANPOWER. The number of men whose strength and/or capabilities are available.

MANSARD. A curb roof having the lower slope almost vertical and the uppermost portion almost flat or horizontal, with the same profile on all four sides of the building.

MANUFACTURE. (1) To make a product. (2) The product itself.

MARGINAL LAND. Land so poor as to remain unused until the lack of more desirable land forces its development.

MARKET STUDY. A survey to determine the present and potential demand for a product or products.

MARKET VALUE. (1) The value of property at present sale. (2) The highest price which a buyer who is willing, but not compelled to buy, will pay, and the lowest price a seller who is willing, but not compelled to sell, will accept.

MARKETABLE TITLE. A clear title free from any cloud or claim.

MARQUEE. A canopy used as a sidewalk shelter at the front of a building.

MARSHALLING. When a creditor has two or more funds out of which to satisfy a debt, he cannot elect to pay so as to deprive another who has but one fund with security.

MARSHALLING YARD. An area in which goods are collected for shipment such as logs, mine props, etc.

MASONITE. A tough fibreboard made from wood fibres.

MATERIAL. That of which anything is or may be composed or constructed.

MATERIEL. Military material.

MATRIX. A rectangular array of numbers and terms enclosed between double vertical bars to facilitate the study of relationships.

MATTE. An impure metallic product in smelting nonferrous metals.

MATURITY. (1) Time fixed for payment. (2) Due date.

MCF. 1,000 cubic feet.

MEAN. (1) The quantity contained within a range or set of numbers or quantities. (2) An average. (3) The sum of a set of numbers divided by the number of terms in the set.

MEANDER. Wandering; winding, especially in the course of a stream.

MECHANIC'S LIEN. A lien against a property owner for material and work performed by another.

MEDIAL. In the middle; the mean.

MEDIAN. (1) Middle, medial. (2) Middle point in a series of values (e.g., 8 is the median number of 2,5,8,10,13; the *mean* would be 7.6).

MEGATON. One million tons.

MEGAWATT. One thousand kilowatts.

MENAGE. A domestic establishment; a household.

MENSURATION. The art of act of measuring.

MERCANTILE AGENCY. A firm that assembles and furnishes information to regular commercial clients, including such data as credit ratings.

MERCANTILE PAPER. Negotiable commercial paper originating solely in regular buying and selling transactions.

MERCANTABLE. (1) Fit to market or sell. (2) Sound.

MERCHANDISE CAR. A railroad car containing less carload shipments.

MERGER. (1) The extinguishment of a lesser estate liability with a greater one. (2) The combining of two or more corporations into one company.

MESA. A high, broad tableland with sharp descending slopes to a surrounding plain.

MESNE. Between two periods or extremes; intermediate.

MESSUAGE. A dwelling with outbuildings and land; the total real estate.

METALLURGY. The science of extracting metals from ores or working with metals to improve their attributes.

METE. (1) A boundary; a limit. (2) To deal or pass on.

METER. 39.37 inches.

METES AND BOUNDS. The limiting boundaries of a property by certain objects. A deed description in which boundaries are defined by directions and distances rather than through actual survey. *Metes* are measurements of length; *bounds* are artificial and natural boundaries such as roads, adjoining properties, streams, etc.

METIER. One's occupation or profession; forte.

METOPE. A square slab in a Doric frieze.

METRIC SYSTEM. A system of weights and measures. The *metric system* is relatively easy to learn because it is a decimal system based entirely on the number 10. The basic measurement of length is the meter, slightly more than a yard. The liter, about 5 percent more than a quart, is used for volume, and the gram is the basic measurement of weight. One must remember to multiply or divide by the powers of ten. For example, for units smaller than a meter, the prefixes are deci (tenths) centi (hundreds) and milli (thousands.) Hence, a tenth of a meter is a decimeter; a hundredth is a centimeter; and a thousandth is a millimeter. For measurements larger than a meter, the prefixes are deka (deca) hecto and kilo. Ten meters becomes dekameter, and so on. (See the Handbook section for tables and U.S. equavalents.) "Metrication" is the ability to produce a line of goods which will be acceptable in foreign "metric system" countries throughout the world.

METRIC TON. One thousand kilograms. (2,204.62 pounds.)

METROPOLITAN AREA. The area including and surrounding a large urban seat used as a center for trading, employment, etc.

MEW. A narrow street or alley with homes fronting on it which often have been converted from stables or private garages.

MHO. The practical unit of electrical conductance. The reciprocal of the ohm.

MIASMA. Obnoxious emanation or atmosphere.

MICA. Isinglass.

MICROCOSM. (1) Small world. (2) A small system regarded as representing a general situation.

MICROINCH. One-millionth of an inch.

MIDDLE ATLANTIC STATES. New York, New Jersey, Pennsylvania.

MIDDLE WEST; MIDWEST. The section of the United States between the Rocky Mountains and the Alleghenies and north of the Ohio River and the southern border of Kansas and Missouri.

MIGRANT WORKER. An itinerant laborer usually moving from state to state to harvest various crops.

MILE. (1) A *statute mile* = 5,280 feet; 1,760 yards. (2) An *international mile* by sea 6,076.103 feet; 1,852 meters. (3) A *nautical* or geographic mile by air or sea = 6,080.2 feet; 1/60 degree of the earth's equator.

MILIEU. Environment; surroundings; arena of activity.

MILLING-IN-TRANSIT. A freight rate permitting shipment of grain from point A to point B at which point the grain is "milled" and the shipment continues to final destination C. The rate is the through rate from A to C of the final commodity and is usually less than the combination of A to B plus B to C.

MILLPOND. A body of water dammed up to supply power for the operation of a mill or factory.

MILLRACE. The current of water that operates a mill water wheel.

MILLSTONE. A thick, heavy stone disk used for grinding.

MILLSTREAM. The water in a mill race.

MILL WHEEL. The water wheel that drives a mill.

MILLWRIGHT. One who plans, builds or maintains mill machinery.

MINARET. A high, slender tower.

MINIMUM RATE. The lowest lawful rate that can be charged for transporting a shipment of goods.

MINIMUM WAGE. The lowest hourly pay rate set by law.

MINIMUM WEIGHT. The lowest poundage upon which a carload or truckload freight rate may be based.

MINSTER. A monastery church.

MISFEASANCE. (1) The performance of a lawful act in an unlawful or culpable manner. (2) Failure to perform in accordance with laws and regulations governing an operation.

MISNOMER. Wrongly named; mis-named.

MIXED LADING. A carload or truckload of different commodities combined into a single shipment.

MIZZENMAST. In a three-masted vessel, the mast nearest the stern. In a vessel having more than three masts, the *mizzen* is third from the bow. In a ketch or yawl, it is the shorter of the two masts.

MOCK-UP. A full-scale model.

MOIETY. (1) Any portion or share. (2) A half share.

MOLYBDENUM. A hard chromium ore used to harden steel.

MONEL METAL. (Trademark.) A nickel alloy containing copper, iron, and manganese used for industrial machine parts.

MONEY OF ACCOUNT. The denomination used in keeping accounts not represented by actual coinage (e.g., the U.S. mill).

MONITOR ROOF. A flat-topped roof raised in the middle to allow installation of craneways and passage of a traveling crane, usually windowed in order to permit daylight to enter into the building.

MONTAGE. (1) A rapid sequence of images to illustrate a group of associated ideas. (2) A picture made by superimposing a number of different pictorial elements.

MONUMENTS. In rural areas, where an exact survey may not be feasible because of excessive cost or other reasons, the description of the property is expressed as "so many acres, *more or less,* or *plus or minus.*" This type of expression is referred to as *monuments.*

MOOT. Debatable; a point for discussion or argument.

MOOT COURT. A court for the trial of a hypothetical legal case or cases by law students.

MOQUETTE. A woolen fabric with velvet-like pile used in carpets and upholstery.

MORAINE. Debris in various forms that has been carried by a glacier (usually in the form of sand and gravel and rocks).

MORASS. (1) A tract of low-lying land. (2) A marsh; bog; swamp.

MORATORIUM. A suspension (of payments, etc.).

MOREEN. A sturdy ribbed fabric used for clothing, upholstery, etc.

MORRIS PLAN BANK. A bank organized to extend small loans to industrial wage earners, and to pay interest on deposits.

MORTGAGE. A conditional transfer of property pledged as security for the payment of money or debt.

MORTGAGE, BLANKET. Where a mortgage is given to include more than one parcel of property, the mortgagee cannot be required to release any part from his *blanket* until payment in full is made for all the properties involved.

MORTGAGE, CHATTEL. A mortgage on personalty such as household goods, appliances, automobile, etc.

MORTGAGE, CLOSED. A mortgage which cannot be prepaid unless the mortgagee accedes to such request (usually with penalty).

MORTGAGE DEED. A deed spelling out the nature of the mortgage.

MORTGAGEE. One to whom the mortgage has been given; the lender.

MORTGAGEE IN POSSESSION. A creditor who takes over the income from a mortgaged property upon default by the debtor.

MORTGAGE FINANCING. The borrowing of funds by loan on property.

MORTGAGE, INDUSTRIAL PROPERTY. A mortgage covering not only real estate, but also fixtures and equipment, even those fixtures added to the property subsequent to the mortgage execution date.

MORTGAGE, OPEN. A mortgage which may be paid off at any time and usually without penalty for prior payment.

MORTGAGOR. An owner who mortgages his property to another.

MORTISE. A space hollowed out in a piece of timber, etc., and shaped to fit a tenon to which it is to be joined; the "female" portion of *tenon and mortise*.

MORTMAIN. The holding of real estate in perpetual ownership (such as a cemetery lot or property under ownership of religious or charitable organizations).

MOUNTAINOUS TERRAIN. Any combination of gradients or lengths of grade that causes trucks to operate at "crawl" speed for a considerable distance or at frequent intervals.

MUCK. Mire; mud.

MULCH. Any loose material placed around plants to protect roots from drying, freezing, etc.

MULE. (1) A small tractor used in warehouses to pull two-axle house trucks or dollies. (2) A yard tractor for towing outside warehouses or factories. (3) A small yard locomotive.

MULLION. A vertical dividing piece in an opening such as a window.

MULLOCK. Waste rock or earth left from a mining operation.

MULTIPARA. A female who has borne more than one child or is carrying a second.

MULTIPLE LISTING. Exchange of property listings between real estate brokers as a result of which commissions are divided between the broker bringing in the listing and the broker making the sale.

MULTIPLE OCCUPANCY. Tenancy or ownership whereby two or more parties occupy a building.

MULTIPLE TENANCY. Occupancy of land or building by more than one occupant under lease.

MUNICIPALITY. An incorporated community.

MUTUAL INSURANCE. A method of insuring in which all policyholders are members of the company contracting to indemnify one another against designated losses.

MUTUAL FUND, CLOSED-END. A fund having a set amount of capital stock and hence issuing no new shares.

MUTUAL FUND, OPEN-END. A fund which may issue additional shares as demand requires.

MUTUAL SAVINGS BANK. A savings bank having no capital and sharing its profits with its depositors.

MUTULE. One of a series of projecting rectangular blocks in a Doric cornice.

N

N.A. (1) Not available. (2) Not applicable.

NACHELLE. An enclosure on an airplane (especially for an engine).

NADIR. The lowest point.

NARROWS. A strait.

NARROWS, THE. A strait connecting Upper New York Bay with Lower New York Bay between the western end of Long Island and Staten Island.

NATATORIUM. An indoor swimming pool.

NATIONAL BANK. A commercial bank chartered by the federal government.

NATURAL CEMENT. Finely pulverized product resulting from the calcination of an argillaceous limestone at a temperature only sufficient to drive off the carbonic acid gas.

NATIONAL PARK. Land preserved by the federal government for recreational, cultural, and scientific uses and not available for purchase by the public.

NATURAL GAS. A gas consisting mostly of methane generated naturally in underground oil deposits.

NAUTICAL MILE. 6,080.2 feet; 1/60 of a degree of the earth's equator. An *international nautical mile* is 1,852 meters; 6,076.103 feet.

NAVE. (1) The main body of a church. (2) The hub of a wheel.

NEAP TIDE. The minimal rise and fall of tide usually after the first and third quarters of the moon when the moon has the least effect upon the tides.

NEGATE. To void; nullify.

NEGOTIABLE. That which may be legally transferred to another party by endorsement or delivery.

NEIGHBORHOOD. Any area considered distinct from other areas; usually a small populated district.

NEPOTISM. Favoritism; especially patronage extended toward relatives.

NESS. A cape; promontory.

NET INCOME. Income before interest charges minus interest charges, plus or minus extraordinary items.

NET LEASE. A lease of property charges normally incurred by the ownership.

NET LISTING. A price which must be agreed upon below which the owner will not sell the property and at which price the broker receives no commission. The broker receives any excess over and above the *net listing* price.

NET TON. A short; ton; 2,000 pounds.

NET WORTH. All legal assets less indebtedness.

NEVE. Granular snow.

NEWEL. The terminal post on the handrail of a staircase.

NEW OPERATION. A new and different production by either a new company or an existing firm in a new or existing facility.

NEW PLANT. A plant to be operated by a company new to a particular location. The operation may be carried on in either a new building or an existing facility.

NEWSPRINT. The paper on which a newspaper is printed.

NEXT FRIEND. One who, although not a guardian, appears to prosecute an action in behalf of some one under legal disability.

NEXT OF KIN. (1) The kindred of a person who would share in his estate. (2) The person most closely related to one.

NEXUS. (1) A bond or tie between several members of a group. (2) A connected series.

NIGHT LATCH. A spring latch operated outside by a key; inside by a knob or lever.

NIGHT SOIL. Contents of outdoors privies, cesspools, etc.

NISI PRIUS. Unless before.

NO-ACCESS ROAD. A road permitting access only at designated interchanges especially constructed for the purpose, as an Interstate highway.

NODE. (1) A knot or knob. (2). The central point; a city or other concentrated subdivision designated as a central location.

NOIBN. Not otherwise indexed by number. (Reference indicated in commodity descriptions in freight classification tariffs.)

NOIL. Short fibre combed out during the preparation of yarns.

NOISOME. (1) Offensive or disgusting. (2) Injurious.

NOLENS VOLENS. Willy nilly.

NOLLE PROSEQUI. An entry in a legal case signifying that the plaintiff will not press the case.

NOLO CONTENDERE. A plea by the defendant which is in effect an admission of guilt but does not bar him from denying the truth of the charges in any other proceeding. Usually places the defendant ''at the mercy of the court.''

NOMINAL. (1) In name only. (2) Trifling; inconsiderable.

NONAGON. Nine-sided.

NONCARRIER. Physical property of a transportation company neither used not held for transportation services (e.g., downtown real estate held for investment or income purposes).

NONCONFORMING USE. An existing property use which does not meet the requirements of the zoning ordinance at the time the ordinance was adopted and therefore does not conform to those regulations. Upon sale, or change of ownership, this exception is usually lost and future use must conform to proper zoning.

NONILLION. A thousand octillion (1 followed by 30 zeros).

NONJOINDER. An omission to join in an action or suit by a person who should be party to such.

NON PROSEQUITUR. To be unwilling to prosecute.

NON SEQUITUR. An irrelevant conclusion.

NON SKED. Non-scheduled airline.

NONUPLE. Having nine parts; ninefold.

NO-PAR STOCK. Stock issued without a face value and sold at whatever price it will command.

NORIA. A waterwheel.

NORM. The pattern or standard regarded as typical of a particular group.

NOS. Not otherwise specified. (Found in some tariffs and product classifications.)

NOTA BENE. Note well; an important notation.

NOTE. A written promise to pay.

NOVATION. Substitution of an old obligation for a new one (As by transferring a debt from one creditor to another.).

NTH DEGREE. (1) Infinitely or indefinitely large or small. (2) Most extreme.

NUDUM PACTUM. A contract made without monetary consideration.

NUISANCE GROUND. A trash dumping area.

O

OASIS. Any place of shelter or relief; a refuge.

OBLIGEE. The person to whom one is obligated; a creditor.

OBLIGOR. The person who is bound to perform an obligation.

OBSOLESCENCE. Impairment of desirability and usefulness brought about by age, physical, economic, fashion, or other changes.

OBSOLETE. Outmoded; out-of-date.

OBTEST. (1) To invoke as a witness. (2) To protest. (3) To beseech; implore.

OCCUPANCY. (1) The act of taking possession of something unowned so as to become its owner. (2) The condition of being an occupant or tenant.

OCTANT. ⅛ part of a circle.

OFFAL. (1) Waste parts of a butchered animal. (2) Rubbish.

OFFSET. A bend or curve in a pipe, etc., to allow clearance around another object.

OGEE. A molding having in profile a long S-curve.

OGIVE. (1) A diagonal rib or a vaulted arch or bay. (2) A pointed arch. (3) A frequency curve any of whose ordinates expresses a number of observations.

OHM. The unit of electrical resistance equal to the resistance of a conductor carrying a current of one ampere at a potential difference of one volt between the terminals.

OOLITE. A variety of limestone resembling fish roe.

OPEN DUMPING. Dumping of waste above ground.

OPEN-END INVESTMENT COMPANY. An investment company which may issue stock shares according to demand.

OPEN-HEARTH FURNACE. A shallow reverberating furnace open at each end to admit fuel and air permitting close control of the finished metal product.

OPEN-HEARTH PROCESS. The conversion of solid pig iron with the addition of iron or steel scrap to steel through exposure to burning gases in the furnace.

OPEN LISTING. An oral or general listing.

OPEN MORTGAGE. A mortgage which may be paid off at any time before maturity, usually without penalty.

OPEN SHOP. (1) An establishment employing both union and nonunion workers. (2) An establishment policy through which only nonunion labor is employed.

OPEN TARE. Actual weight.

OPEN-TIMBER. A forest having little or no undergrowth.

OPERATING EXPENSES. A group of expenses applicable to operations (e.g., maintenance, taxes, depreciation, etc.).

OPERATING INCOME. Revenue from operations less expenses incurred in operations.

OPPIDAN. Civic; relating to the community.

OPTION. The purchased privilege of either buying or selling something at a specified price within a specified time.

ORDINANCE. A law; decree; regulation.

ORDINARY. In some states, a judge exercising probate jurisdiction.

ORDINATE. The distance of any point from one axis measured by a line parallel to another axis.

ORDNANCE. Military material.

ORDONNANCE. Any code of laws.

ORIENT. To adjust; make familiar with surroundings or subject.

ORIGINAL COST TO DATE. Cost of original purchase and/or construction plus all additional costs for expansion or improvements, less credit for the portion of the property retired.

ORPHAN. (1) A child whose both parents are dead. (2) Less commonly, a child with but one surviving parent.

OSCILLATE. (1) To swing back and forth on a pendulum. (2) To waver or fluctuate. (3) To spin. (4) To vibrate.

OSMOSIS. The diffusion of a liquid through a semipermeable membrane resulting in equalization of pressure on both sides.

OUSTER. The act of putting one out of possession of real property to which he may be legally entitled.

OUTAGE. The failure of electric power.

OUTBUILDING. A structure separate and subordinate to the main building (e.g., a shed or barn).

OUTCROP. The exposure of any rock or rock stratum at or above the surface of the ground.

OUTHOUSE. An outdoor privy or outbuilding.

OUTLAND. The outlying regions of a county; a hinterland.

OUTLIER. An exposed mass of rock surrounded by older or underlying rock strata that have been worn down by erosion or denudation.

OUTLYING BUSINESS DISTRICT. (1) A shopping center at the edge of a community. (2) The portion of a municipality or area within its influence separated by some distance from the central business district and its fringe areas in which the principal land use is for business activity.

OVERBURDEN. That portion of soil overlying a rock strata or a desired level of operation.

OVERCAPITALIZE. To invest capital to an extent not warranted by actual value or future prospects.

OVERCROP. To exhaust the fertility of soil by "one-cropping."

OVERDUE. Past due; late.

OVERHEAD. The operating expenses that cannot be attributed to any one division of a business such as rent, heat, light, taxes.

OVER-IMPROVEMENT. An improvement which is not the best use for the site on which it is located because of excess size or cost.

OVER-THE-COUNTER STOCK. A stock not sold on the floor of a stock exchange and therefore a stock or bond not listed by any recognized stock exchange.

OWNERSHIP. Legal title; proprietorship.

OYER. A copy of a document sued upon given by the party holding the document to the party being sued.

OZARKS. The hilly uplands of Missouri, Arkansas, and Oklahoma.

P

PACE. A stride of three feet.

PACHYSANDRA. (1) A hardy evergreen cultivated for ground cover. (2) A shade grass.

PACKAGE CAR. A railroad car containing several less than carload shipments; a merchandise car.

PACKAGE DEAL. A key-in-the-lock arrangement whereby an entrepreneur, realtor, or builder, or others offers to purchase a site, and build and equip a business or industrial plant for a fee. Costs are armortized over a period of years.

PALISADE. An extended cliff or rocky precipice.

PALISADES, THE. The cliffs extending twenty-five miles along the western bank of the Hudson River in New York and New Jersey.

PALLET. A movable platform for the storage or transportation of goods.

PALUDAL. Marshy; swampy.

PANDEMIC. (1) General; universal. (2) Pertaining to all people.

PANTOGRAPH. A trolley or other device for collecting electric power from an overhead conductor for a transportation vehicle.

PAPER. (1) Negotiable evidence. (2) A treatise.

PARAMETER. (1) A constant whose values determine the operations or characteristics of a system. (2) A fixed limit or guide line.

PARAPET. A low wall about the edge of a building's roof.

PARAPHERNALIA. (1) Gear; equipment; personal effects. (2) Formerly, a wife's belongings over and above her dowry.

PARBUCKLE. A device for raising or lowering heavy cylindrical objects, such as a heavy cask along an inclined plane, consisting of a doubled rope securely looped at the top of the incline and passed around the object, the free ends being hauled or played out as desired.

PARCENARY. (1) A coparcenary. (2) An estate in lands inherited in undivided interest by two or more heirs.

PAR EXCELLENCE. Beyond comparison; preeminent.

PAR FLECHE. Rawhide which has been freed of hair by being soaked in lye and stretched to dry.

PARGET. Plaster suitable for lining chimneys.

PARGETING. Plastering, especially stucco work on outside walls.

PARISH. In Louisiana, a governmental district corresponding to a county in other states.

PARKING SPACE. 250 square feet per car for an attended parking lot; unattended, 350 feet. (According to the Society of Industrial Realtors publication *Industrial Real Estate,* about 60 percent of an industrial plant parking area will be used for vehicle storage, while the remaining 40 percent is required for vehicle movement.)

88

PARKWAY. A wide thoroughfare with median strip planted with shrubbery, trees, and grass.

PAROCHIAL. (1) Provincial. (2) Confined. (3) Narrowness of view; akin to chauvinism.

PARQUETRY. Inlaid mosaic of wood.

PARTERRE. (1) A flower garden having its beds arranged in patterns. (2) The part of a theatre under the balcony on the main floor.

PARTICLE BOARD. (1) Chip board usually used for interior walls. (2) A drywall material in which particles of wood or other matter have been imbedded.

PARTICULATE. Any material, other than water, in suspension in the air, such as dust, carbon, chemicals, etc.

PARTITE. Divided into, or composed of parts.

PARTNER. An associate in business who has a financial interest.

PARTNERSHIP. A joint interest and contractural relationship in which two or more persons carry on a business.

PARTY WALL. A wall erected on a line between two adjoining properties and used in common by neighboring owners.

PAR VALUE. The stated value of a stock; face value, distinguished from market value.

PASS. (1) The passage of any piece of metal via the rolls of a rolling mill. (2) A gap through a mountain permitting the passage of people, animals, or vehicles. (3) An instrument permitting free passage or entrance, as a *press pass* allowing reporters to enter an area without payment.

PASSIVE FINANCIAL INSTRUMENTS. Denoting stocks and bonds which bear no interest.

PASTORAL. Pertaining to rural life.

PASTURAGE. Ground suitable for grazing.

PATENTEE. One who holds a patent.

PATENTOR. One who grants a patent.

PAUPER. Anyone who is entitled to receive public charity.

PAWL. A pivotal bar adapted to fall into the ratchets or teeth of a wheel as it rotates in one direction and restrains it from backward slippage.

PAYEE. A person to whom payment is made.

PAYER. One who pays.

PAYLOAD. The part of the cargo producing revenue to the carrier.

PEAT. A partially carbonized vegetable tissue used as fuel.

PEAVEY. A cant hook with the end sharpened as a spike.

PECULIUM. Private property.

PEDIMENT. A broad triangular part above a portico or door.

PEDOSPHERE. The soil-bearing layer of the earth's surface.

PENDENT. (1) Suspended. (2) Projecting; overhanging.

PENDENTE LITE. Pending, or during a legal suit.

PENEPLAIN. An area worn down by erosion until it resembles a plain.

PENETRATION RESISTANCE. The resistance of soil to erosion. (Used to determine weight-bearing qualities of the soil as well as percolation features.)

PENTAD. A group of five.

PENTAGON. A five-sided figure.

PENTAGON, THE. The building housing the Department of Defense.

PENTHOUSE. (1) An apartment or dwelling on the roof of a building. (2) A structure on the roof of a building to cover a water tank, elevator shaft, machinery, etc. (3) A canopy or awning above a window or doorway.

PER ANNUM. Yearly; by the year.

PER CAPITA. Per person; for each; by heads.

PERCENTAGE. (1) Rate per hundred. (2) Commission rate.

PERCENTAGE LEASE. The lease of a property in which rental is based upon volume of sales on the leased premises.

PERCENTILE. Any of 100 points spaced at equal intervals within the range of a plotted variable. (Thus, 1,2,3, etc., percentage of the cases are in the first, second, third, etc., *percentile*.)

PERCH. 16 ½ feet.

PERCOLATION. The act of water descending through the earth from the ground surface.

PER DIEM. By the day; per day.

PERFORMANCE STANDARDS. The technique of judging an industry in terms of the effect it has on the surrounding environment, including tests of smoke concentration, dust control, noise factors, noisome odors, etc. (Definite measurements to determine the effect of a particular use within predetermined limits and therefore to rule it permissible in a particular zoned area.)

PERIMETER. (1) The boundary line of any two-dimensional figure. (2) The sides of a plane figure. (3) The bounds of a plane figure.

PERIMORPH. A mineral that encloses another.

PERIPHERAL. Marginal; not central.

PERIPHERY. (1) The outer part, surface or boundary of something. (2) A surrounding region, area or country.

PERIPTERAL. Having a row of columns around all sides of a building.

PERISTYLE. A system of columns about a building or internal court.

PERMEABLE. Allowing passage of fluids.

PERMEANCE. The ability to be traversed by magnetic lines of force.

PERPEND. In masonry, a stone extending through a wall so that an end of the stone appears on each side of the wall.

PERPETUITY. Forever.

PERSONAL EFFECTS. Clothing and other personal, private property.

PERSONALTY. Personal property.

PERSONA GRATA. A welcome person.

PERSONA NON GRATA. A person who is neither welcome nor acceptable.

PETIT JURY. (1) A petty jury. (2) A jury that sits at a trial in civil and criminal cases. (3) A trial jury.

PEWTER. An alloy of tin and lead.

PH. A symbol denoting the negative logarithm of the hydrogen iron concentration in grams per liter of a solution; used in expressing relative acidity and alkalinity—hardness. (A pH of 7 is regarded as neutral.)

PHOTOGRAMMETRY. The technique of making surveys or maps by means of aerial photographs.

PHOTO MAP. A map composed of one or more aerial photographs.

PI. The ratio of the circumference of a circle to its diameter; 3.1416.

PIECE GOODS. Fabrics sold from bolts of cloth in lengths desired by the customer.

PIECE RATES. Rates paid to workers based on the number of units produced by the worker.

PIECE WORK. Work done and paid for by the number of units produced.

PIE FACTORS. Population, Investment, Employment.

PIER. (1) An upright projecting portion of a wall. (2) A solid portion of a wall between windows and door openings. (3) Support for adjacent ends of bridge spans. (4) A dock or wharf.

PIGGYBACK TRANSPORTATION. The mode of rail/truck transportation in which loaded trailers and containers are transported on railroad flat cars.

PIG IRON. The product, either cast or in molten state, resulting from heating iron ore, limestone and coke together in a blast furnance. Pig iron contains carbon ranging from 3 percent to 4 percent.

PILASTER. A rectangular column engaged in a wall.

PILE. A heavy timber of metal or concrete pole forced into the earth to form a foundation for a building or other structure.

PILING. Piles, collectively.

PILLAR. (1) A vertical, free-standing support. (2) A column. (3) A shaft.

PINCH BAR. A crowbar with a short projection for prying forward heavy objects.

PINCHBECK. (1) An alloy cf copper, zinc, tin forming a cheap imitation of gold. (2) Cheap. (3) Spurious.

PINION. A toothed wheel driving, or driven, by a larger cog.

PIRN. A small spindle.

PITCHBLENDE. The chief source of uranium; a black (or brown) variety of uranite.

PLACER. An alluvial or glacial deposit of sand, gravel, etc., containing gold in particles large enough to be recovered by panning or washing.

PLAFOND. A flat or arched ceiling usually ornately carved.

PLAINTIFF. The complainant or suer in an action.

PLANCH. A board or plank.

PLANTATION. (1) Any place that is planted. (2) A farm of many acres. (3) A grove cultivated and planted for its wood. (4) An oyster bed.

PLASTERBOARD. A board made of a slab of gypsum mixed with fibres or of plaster between sheets of fibrous paper, used as wallboard.

PLAT. A plotted map, chart, or plan, as a *property plat*.

PLAT BOOK. A public record of property plats and ownership.

PLATEAU. (1) A mesa. (2) An extensive stretch of elevated, level land.

PLATE GLASS. Clear glass in thick sheets suitable for store windows, mirrors, and the like.

PLATFORM CAR. A railroad flat car.

PLEBISCITE. (1) An expression of the popular will of the people by means of a vote of the whole people. (2) A referendum.

PLEXIGLAS. (Trademark.) A lightweight thermoplastic acrylic resin, transparent and weather resistant.

PLINTH. A slab, block, or stone on which a column, pedestal, or statue rests.

PLOT. A piece of ground used for special purposes.

PLOTTAGE. Assemblage of small ownerships into a single ownership.

PLUMB. (1) The lead weight on the end of a line used to find the exact perpendicular. (2) A lead weight to sound the depth of water.

PLUMB BOB. The weight used at the end of a plumb line; a plumb.

PLUMB LINE. The cord from which the plumb bob is suspended.

PLUMMET. A plumb bob.

PLUVIOMETER. A rain gauge.

PLYWOOD. A structural material consisting of an odd number of layers of wood glued together, usually at right angles, to give added strength.

PNEUMATIC. Containing air or gas.

POACH. (1) To become soft and muddy by being trampled. (2) To sink into mud or soft earth while walking.

POACHY. Swampy; soft; mirey.

PODIUM. (1) A solid foundation supporting a structure. (2) A small platform or dais for a speaker.

POGONIP. A cold fog containing ice particles, found particularly in the Sierra Nevadas.

POINTING. Filling the joints and/or defects in the face of a masonry structure.

POINT OF SWITCH. That end of the railroad switch rail farthest from the frog.

POINT OF TANGENT (PT). The point at which a railroad spur or sidetrack takes off from the curve of the main track.

POINTS. The charge made for obtaining funding for a client, usually expressed in *percentage points* and commonly used with respect to housing mortgages.

POLDER. A tract of marshy land that has been reclaimed by the erection of dikes.

POLE. A perch; 16 ½ feet.

POLICE POWER. The inherent right of a government to pass such legislation as may be required to protect the public health and safety and to promote the general welfare.

POLITICAL SUBDIVISION. A governmental entity smaller than the whole.

POLYGON. A plane figure enclosed by straight sides.

POOL CAR. (1) A railroad car in which freight from a number of shippers is consolidated for delivery at a common destination point. (2) Specially equipped car of more than one ownership assigned to a specific company or location.

POPULACE. The masses.

PORK BARREL. Federal appropriation for some local project that will favorably impress a government representative's constituency.

POROSITY. The property of being permeable by fluids.

PORT. (1) The left side of a boat as one faces forward. (2) A place where customs clearance is available. Does not need to be connected with a body of water; a port of entry. (3) A harbor or haven.

PORTAL-TO-PORTAL PAY. A wage computed on full time spent on company property from arrival to departure regardless of the amount of production or activity of workers.

PORT AUTHORITY. An official body having charge of the coordination of all traffic of a port.

PORTICO. (1) A stoa. (2) An open space with roof upheld by columns usually as a canopy over a doorway opening on a drive.

PORT OF ENTRY. A place on the seacoast, or inland, designated as a point at which persons or merchandise may enter or leave a country under the supervision of customs laws.

POSITRON. An antiparticle corresponding to an electron.

POSSE COMITATUS. A body of men called by a peace officer to assist him in his work; a posse.

POSTERIOR. Later; subsequent; behind.

POSTHUMOUS. (1) Continuing after one's death. (2) A child born after its father's death.

POST MORTEM. After death.

POSTPARTUM. After childbirth.

POSTPONEMENT OF LIEN. The subordination of a presently prior lien to a subsequent judgment or mortgage.

POUNDAGE. (1) The act of impounding cattle. (2) The charges for the redemption of the impounded cattle.

POUNDAL. A unit of force that, acting on a one-pound mass, changes its velocity by one foot per second, per second.

POWER FACTOR. The ratio of the real power (kilowatts) to apparent power (kilovoltamperes) for any given load and time, expressed as a percentage ratio.

POWER OF ATTORNEY. The authority to act conferred on an agent; the document authorizing such power.

PRAGMATISM. The doctrine that ideas have value only in terms of their practical consequences or results.

PRAXIS. (1) Practical. (2) Accepted or habitual practice regardless of expected actions as set forth ''by the book.''

PREDILECTION. A bias in favor of something; partiality.

PREEMPT. (1) To acquire beforehand. (2) To occupy public land so as to acquire property by *preemption*.

PREEMPTION. The right to purchase or claim before others.

PREFABRICATE. To manufacture in standard sections for ease in assembly on location.

PREFERENTIAL SHOP. A shop that gives preferential treatment to union members.

PREFERRED STOCK. Stock on which dividends must be paid prior to common stock. In the event of liquidation, preferential treatment in the distribution of assets is accorded *preferred* stockholders.

PREMISE. A proposition that serves as ground for a conclusion.

PREMISES. A definite portion of real estate.

PREMIUM. (1) The amount of bonus paid for a loan in addition to normal interest charges; points. (2) The payments required to maintain an insurance policy.

PREPAYMENT LOAN CONDITIONS. The terms by which a loan may be paid prior to the maturity date.

PRESCRIBE. To render invalid by lapse of time.

PRICE-EARNINGS RATIO (P/E). Market price divided by the annual earnings per share of common stock.

PRETERITION. The omission of a natural heir in a will.

PRIMA FACIE. (1) At first view. (2) Evident or self-evident.

PRIMA FACIE EVIDENCE. Evidence if unexplained and unrefuted would establish the fact alleged.

PRIMAGE. An allowance paid to the owner of a vessel in addition to freight charges for taking care of, or tending, goods during shipment.

PRIMARY ENERGY. Energy available from firm power.

PRIME COST. The direct cost of labor and materials in production exclusive of capital and overhead expenses.

PRIME MOVER. The engine, turbine, water wheel, etc., which drives an electric generator.

PRINCIPAL. (1) Property or capital as opposed to interest or income. (2) The most important truss or rafter of a roof. (3) The seller of property who is primarily liable for breach of contract, etc. (4) Chief or primary.

PRINCIPAL NOTE. The promissory note which is secured by the mortgage or trust deed.

PRINCIPIUM. First principle; beginning; fundamental.

PRINCIPLE. A general truth; that which is inherent.

PRIVATE CARRIER. A company which maintains its own trucks to transport its own freight.

PROBATE. Formal, legal proof (e.g., a will).

PROBATE COURT. A court having jurisdiction over the proof of wills, etc.

PROFILE. (1) The outline of a perpendicular section of a building. (2) A brief description of a will, property, report, or person.

PRO FORMA. (1) As a matter of form. (2) An estimate of anticipated income, profits, etc.

PROGRAM. (1) A proposed or prearranged plan or course of proceedings. (2) A sequence of instructions set up in an electronic computer. (3) A prefatory statement.

PROMISSORY NOTE. A written promise to repay a certain amount of money at a specified time with specified rate of interest.

PROMONTORY. A high point of land extending into the sea.

PROPANE. A fuel gas obtained from petroleum.

PROPERTY. (1) Any object of any value. (2) A parcel of land.

PROPERTY MAP. A plat map indicating lots or other land ownership.

PROPINQUITY. (1) Nearness in time or place. (2) Kinship.

PROPRIETARY. (1) Subject to exclusive ownership. (2) Designating an article, such as a drug, protected as to name or process by copyright, patent, etc.

PRO RATA. In proportion.

PRORATE. To divide proportionately.

PROSCRIBE. Prohibit; outlaw; ostracize; reject with condemnation, as a doctrine or practice.

PROSELYTIZE. (1) To convert. (2) To endeavor to bring industry into an area by solicitation. (3) To relocate an industrial plant by special inducements such as tax relief, free site, etc.

PROSPECT. A company definitely interested in locating a new or expanded operation in the area of interest to the developer.

PROSPECTUS. (1) A paper containing information of a proposed industrial undertaking. (2) A summary; outline; pro forma. (3) A printed presentation for a new enterprise, such as a property subdivision, stock offering, etc.

PROTECTIVE COVENANTS. Restrictions in leases or deeds to maintain the quality of a planned industrial area, including such items as uses, nuisances, building plans and materials, set-back lines, location of loading and parking areas, landscaping, etc.; *restrictive covenants*.

PROTECTIVE TARIFF. A tariff designed to protect domestic industries against foreign competition.

PRO TEMPORE. (1) For the time being. (2) Temporary.

PROTHONOTARY. A probate officer.

PROTON. One of the elementary particles in the nucleus of an atom.

PROTOTYPE. An original model on which subsequent forms are to be based.

PROTRACTOR. An instrument for measuring and laying off angles.

PROVINCIAL. (1) Narrow. (2) Parochial.

PROXIMITY. Nearness; closeness; next to.

PROXY. A person empowered to act for another; a delegate.

PUBLIC DOMAIN. (1) Lands owned by the state or federal government. (2) Public lands.

PUBLIC TRUSTEE. A person appointed or required by law to execute a trust.

PUBLIC UTILITY DISTRICT. A political subdivision embracing an area wider than a single municipality or county for the purpose of generating, transmitting, and distributing electric energy.

PUBLISHING AGENT. A person authorized by transportation lines to publish tariffs.

PUDDLER. (1) A device for stirring molten or fused metals. (2) A person who operates such a device.

PUG. A machine in which clay is ground, mixed, and tempered.

PULPWOOD. The soft wood of certain trees used in the manufacture of paper.

PUNCHEON. A liquor cask of varying capacity from 72 to 120 gallons.

PUNTY. An iron rod used in glass making to handle hot glass.

PURCHASE MONEY MORTGAGE. (1) A document given by the buyer to the seller in part payment of the purchase price of the real estate. (2) Evidence that indebtedness secured by a mortgage represents the purchase price of the described real estate.

PURLIEU. The outlying districts; outskirts; environs.

PURLIN. A horizontal timber supporting rafters.

PURLOIN. To steal.

PURVEYANCE. Provisions; food.

PURVIEW. (1) Extent, sphere or scope, as of official authority. (2) The body or scope or limit of a statute or regulation.

PYLON. (1) One of the steel towers supporting a high tension electric power line.

PYREX. (Trademark.) A type of heat-resistant glass having a high silica content with additions of soda, aluminum, and boron.

PYRITES. Any of various metallic sulphides.

PYROSTAT. A thermostat adapted to extraordinarily high temperatures.

Q

QUADRANT. (1) A quarter section of a circle. (2) A quarter sector.

QUADRATURE. The determination of the area of a curved surface.

QUADRILATERAL. Four-sided.

QUADRIPARTITE. (1) Having four parts. (2) A four-party agreement.

QUANTUM THEORY. The theory that energy is not a smoothly flowing continuance but is manifested by the emission from radiating bodies of discrete particles or *quanta*.

QUARTER SECTION. One-quarter of a section; a tract of land one-half mile square; 160 acres.

QUASI. Resembling but not genuine.

QUASI-CONTRACT. An obligation enforceable by contract but imposed by operation of law regardless of the consent of the defendant.

QUAY. A wharf or landing place for loading and unloading vessels.

QUEEN POST. One of two upright suspending or sustaining posts of compression members as a roof truss.

QUICK ASSETS. Liquid assets capable of being turned into cash.

QUIET ENJOYMENT. The right of an owner to use property without interference of possession.

QUITCLAIM. (1) A full release given by one to another in regard to a certain demand, suit, or right of action. (2) To relinquish or give up claim or title to; release from claim.

QUOIN. (1) The external corner of a building. (2) Any of the large stones by which the corner of the building is marked.

QUOTATIONS. Current prices of stocks and commodities.

QUO WARRANTO. (1) A judicial writ commanding a person to show by what authority he exercises an office or franchise. (2) A proceeding by which a government seeks to recover an office or franchise.

R

RABBET. A groove or cut made in a board so that another piece may be fitted to form a joint.

RACK RENT. Exorbitant rental charges.

RADIANT HEATING. The system in which heat is diffused by radiation from walls, ceiling, or floor.

RADIUS VECTOR. The straight-line distance from a fixed origin to any point in a curve.

RADIX. A number used as the basis of a scale enumeration. (For example, 10 is the *radix* of the common system of logarithms.)

RAFTER. A beam giving support to a roof.

RAILHEAD. (1) A railroad terminus. (2) The farthest point to which rails have been laid on an uncompleted railroad.

RAILWAY. A railroad, but may refer to a trolley system.

RAMPART. A bulwark, levee, or embankment, usually in reference to a military installation.

RANGE. A single series or rows of townships numbered east/west from a base meridian.

RATAL. An amount on which rates are based.

RATIOCINATION. Reasoning.

RATIONALE. The logical basis for a proposition, presentation, or a proposal.

RAW MATERIAL. Unprocessed matter used in manufacturing, such as sand, gravel, wood, etc. Also sometimes refers to supplies from other producers used in the finished product.

REAL ESTATE. Land and improvements together with whatever is attached to the property by man or nature.

REAL POWER. The rate of supply of energy measured in kilowatts. (The product of *real power* and length of time is energy measured by watt-hour meters and expressed in kilowatt-hours.)

REAL PROPERTY. Real estate. The land and appurtenances; realty.

REALTOR. A person engaged in the real estate business who is a member of the National Association of Real Estate Boards.

REALTY. Real estate or real property in any form.

REAL WAGES. Value of income in purchasing power rather than nominal wages.

REBATE. A deduction from the gross amount.

RECEIPT. Written acknowledgment that payment has been made.

RECEIVABLES. Outstanding accounts listed as assets.

RECEIVER. An officer appointed by a court to hold property in trust that is in litigation or to wind up the affairs of a bankrupt company.

RECEIVERSHIP. The state of being in bankruptcy, or in the hands of a receiver.

RECIPROCAL SWITCHING AGREEMENT. An agreement between two or more railroads to switch inbound and outbound carload freight to or from a siding of another carrier under a regular switching charge which normally is absorbed by the carrier receiving the line haul.

RECISION. Annulment; cancellation.

RECONSIGNMENT. The act of consigning goods to other than the original person or place originally ordered while the goods are in shipment or transit. The privilege is extended at the through rate from the initial point to that of the final delivery.

RECONVEY. To convey back to an original owner.

RECORDER OF DEEDS. An officer of a county in charge of recorded deeds and transfers of property, which are available for public inspection.

RECTIFIER. A refiner or compounder of spiritous liquors.

RECTIFY. (1) To correct. (2) To refine by repeated distillations until the desired purity is obtained in a liquid.

RECUPPING. Reforming the head of a rivet after it has been driven.

REDAN. A fortification.

REDEVELOPMENT. Rehabilitation of a deteriorated area of a city by means of razing existing structures and rebuilding the area.

REDOUBT. An enclosed, usually temporary fortification.

REDUCTION. (1) The process of depriving a compound of oxygen. (2) Removal of impurities (from metals.)

REEFER. A refrigerated railroad car or truck for transporting perishable freight.

REEVALUATE. To reconsider or evaluate anew.

REEVE. To pass a rope through a block or pulley.

REFEREE. A person to whom a case is sent by order of a court for investigation and report (e.g., a *referee* in bankruptcy).

REFERENDUM. A vote of the people to determine a course of action.

REFORESTATION. The replanting of trees in an area which has been or is being harvested for its wood.

REFRACTIVE INDFX. The ratio of the velocity of a specific radiation in a vacuum to its velocity in another medium.

REFRACTORY. Resisting heat or ordinary means of reduction of ores.

REFRACTORY BRICK. A clay product specially treated for heat resistance and used in the hearth of a steel furnace.

REFUND. Reimbursement. (Railroads usually require full payment from a firm for the portion of the railroad sidetrack on railroad right-of-way and then *refund* some amount for each carload of road-haul traffic utilized by the firm. The *refund* continues for an agreed number of years or until the industry has been *refunded* for its advance payment, whichever first occurs.)

REGIONAL COMMISSION. A federal-states body created in the 1960s to provide categorical grants, planning, and technical assistance for certain projects directed toward improving the facilities and enhancing the economy of the region.

REGLET. A flat and narrow molding.

REGRESS. To return to the mean value of a series of observations.

REGULUS. An intermediate product resulting from smelting various ores.

REIMBURSEMENT. (1) Refund. (2) Rebate.

REINFORCED CONCRETE. Concrete containing metal bars, rods, or netting to increase its tensile strength and durability.

RELAY. A switch that utilizes variations in the condition or strength of a current in a circuit to effect the operation of similar devices in the same or another circuit (e.g., blinker lights).

RELEVANT. Pertinent; fitting.

RELICT. A widow or widower.

RELIEF MAP. A map in which contours and topography are shown in bas relief.

RELOCATION. The removal of an industrial operation from one community to another (no federal assistance may be provided for such).

RELUCTANCE. Capacity for opposing magnetic induction. (The opposite of permeance.)

REMAND. (1) To order back or send back. (2) To recommit to custody. (3) To send back to a lower court.

REMISE. Give up; surrender; release; relinquish.

RENEWAL. Redevelopment; rehabilitation of a deteriorated area of a community by razing existing structures and rebuilding the area.

RENT. Compensation for use of a property under rental agreement.

RENTAL PROPERTY. Real estate offered for rent or lease.

RENTER. A tenant; one who leases property by paying rent.

REPAIR TRACK. A railroad track on which cars are put for repair.

REPARATION. (1) Atonement. (2) Payment for damages.

REPLEVIN. An action to regain possession of personal property.

REPOSITORY. A depository for goods.

REPRODUCTION COST. The cost to reproduce at prevailing prices.

REPUDIATION. The disowning of a contract or debt.

REQUIREMENTS. Needs (Plant location requirements include: site, availability of labor, utilities, transportation facilities, etc.)

RESERVATION. A tract of land reserved for special purposes such as a game preserve; Indian reservation; park area, etc.)

RESERVE. (1) In banking, the amount of funds *reserved* from outside investment in order to promptly meet regular or emergency demands.

The *reserve* is set by state law as a percentage of assets. (2) An amount set aside for contingent loss, liability, or needs for expansion.

RESERVOIR. A basin, either natural or artificial, for collecting and storing water.

RESIDUAL PRESSURE. The water pressure at the extremities of a water system.

RESIDUAL SOILS. Soils formed by in-place weathering of the underlying rock.

RESIDIUM. Remainder; residual.

RESISTANCE. The opposition that a conductor offers to the passage of a current resulting from the conversion of energy into heat, light, etc., radiated away from the current, expressed in ohms.

RESISTOR. A device for introducing resistance into an electric current.

RESOLUTION. A judgment or decision (e.g. a *zoning resolution*).

RESTITUTION. (1) Restoration of something that had been taken away or lost. (2) Repayment for personal or property damage brought about by a defendant.

RESTORATION. Returning a person or thing to a former condition; rehabilitation; renewal.

RESTRAINT OF TRADE. Interference with the free flow of goods, as by price-fixing.

RESTRICTION. A device in a deed for controlling the use of property after sale.

RESTRICTIVE CONVENANT. (1) Restriction. (2) A clause in a deed limiting the use of property conveyed for a certain period of time.

RETAINER. (1) A device for holding parts of ball or roller bearings in place. (2) A fee paid to a consultant or lawyer to make his services available on call.

RETAINING WALL. A wall to prevent an embankment from sliding.

RETARDER. A braking device built into a railroad track to control the speed of railroad cars being switched in a classification yard.

RETORT. A vessel with bent tube for the heating and/or distillation of liquids.

RETRAINING. The re-education (usually in vocational pursuits) of workers for production work in fields with which they have had little or no experience. Also for the purpose of upgrading workers' capabilities in areas with which they have had some previous training or experience.

RETROACTIVE. An action taking effect at a date or time prior to actual enactment. (A "grandfather clause" or action.)

RETROGRESS. To go back to an earlier and sometimes worse condition.

REVALUATE. To place a different value on.

REVENUE STAMP. A stamp affixed to a product or paper (as a deed) to indicate that a tax has been paid.

REVERBERATORY FURNACE. A furnace having a vaulted roof that deflects the flame downward toward the substance to be treated.

REVERSION. The residue of an estate left to the grantor to commence after the determination of some particular estate granted out by him.

REVETMENT. A facing or sheathing, as of masonry, to protect earthworks, river banks, etc.; a retaining wall.

REVOCATION. Annulment or cancellation of a legal instrument.

REVOLVING FUND. A fund set up for loans to operations that yield returns which in turn are used for further loans and re-use.

RHABDOMANCY. Divining by use of a divining rod; dowsing.

RHEOMETER. A device for indicating the force or velocity of a fluid flow.

RHEOSTAT. A device used to control current and voltage in a current, as for regulating blinker lights.

RIDGE. A long and narrow elevation of land; an arete.

RIDGE POLE. A horizontal timber at the ridge of a roof to which rafters are fastened.

RIGHT-OF-WAY. (1) The strip of land over which a railroad or highway may be built with added land for clearance, abutments, etc. Also a strip over which high tension transmission lines may be built; (2) An easement to allow access to a property.

RIGHT-TO-WORK LAW. A statute outlawing the closed shop.

RILL. A small stream; a rivulet.

RILLET. A small rill.

RIPARIAN RIGHTS. The right of an owner of land along the banks of a stream to use the water in any way that will not deprive others, who are located downstream, of such uses.

RIPRAP. Broken stone loosely thrown together without mortar about the base of bridge piers and abutments to prevent scour on the banks. Utilized for stemming or repairing damage from flood, etc.

RIPTIDE. Conflicting tide or current; undertow.

RIP TRACK. A railroad track for storage of cars in need of repair.

RISK CAPITAL. Money available for enterprises which otherwise could not

RIVER BASIN. An area of land drained by a river and its branches.

RIVERHEAD. The source of a river.

ROADBED. (1) The subgrade (gravel, aggregates, etc.) on which rails and ties of a railroad are laid. (2) The graded foundation or surface of a roadway.

ROAD METAL. Broken stone used for building or repairing roads.

ROADSTEAD. A sheltered off-shore anchorage area.

ROCK ASPHALT. Sandstone or limestone naturally impregnated with asphalt.

ROLLING MILL. A manufacturing operation in which metal is rolled into sheets, bars, etc.

Rolling stock. The wheeled equipment of a transportation company.

Rolling terrain. Any combination of gradients, length of grade, that cause trucks to reduce speed below that of passenger cars on some sections of the highway but which does not involve sustained crawl speed for any substantial distance. (2) Rolling, or level-to-rolling terrain is ideal for industrial site development. Borrow and fill areas are available on site and drainage is good.

Rollway. (1) A chute. (2) An inclined way down which products may be rolled.

Roman arch. A massive semicircular arch.

Roof types. (1) *Flat*. A level roof with a slight gradient to the eaves for drainage. (2) *Gable*. A "hip roof" with ridge pole. (3) *Monitor*. A flat-top roof raised in the middle to allow passage of craneway and windowed to permit the entrance of daylight. (34) *Sawtooth*. A series of sawtooth-like windowed upright roof extensions for the purpose of gaining the best daylight. (Modern-day lighting devices have greatly reduced sawtooth construction methods as too expensive for the benefits received.)

Roomette. A small, single-occupancy enclosed area in a railroad Pullman or sleeping car with bed and lavatory facilities self-contained.; a small bedroom.

Rostrum. Pulpit; platform; dais.

Rotary forms. Forms, such as billings, checks, charge slips, produced in continuous strips or rolls on rotary printing presses.

Rotiform. Shaped like a wheel.

Rotunda. A domed, circular building.

Rubble. Rip-rap; field stone or rough stone as it comes from a quarry.

Rubigo. Red iron oxide used as a polishing powder or pigment.

Rule "G". A railroad operating rule prohibiting the use or possession of intoxicants or narcotics while on duty.

Rule of fifths. (As used by the land developer). One-fifth of the price received for a developed lot without improvements will go the to raw land; 1/5 for improvements (engineering, legal fees, utilities, roads); 1/5 for interest, carrying charges and miscellaneous costs; and 2/5 for administration, advertising, sales costs, commissions, and the developer's profit.

Rundle. (1) A rung (as on a ladder.) (2) Something that turns or rotates about an axle, as the drum of a winch or capstan.

Rundlet. A small barrel with about 18 gallons capacity.

Runlet. A small stream; a rivulet.

Runnel. A small stream; a rivulet; a runlet.

Running track. (1) A railroad track reserved for the movement of equipment through a yard. (2) A track designated in the timetable upon which movements may be subject to signals, and/or rules, special instructions.

RUNOFF. Drainage; the part of the precipitation that is not absorbed by soil but is drained off in rills and streams.

S

SABIN. A measure of sound absorption equal to one square foot of completely absorbing substance.

SACCHAROID. A granular and crystal-like structure similar to a cube of sugar.

SADIRON. A pressing iron pointed at both ends with removable handle.

SAGGAR, SEGGAR. A vessel of baked fireclay into which delicate pieces of pottery are placed to prevent direct exposure to heat.

SALE. Transfer of property for a consideration.

SALE-AND-LEASEBACK. The potential occupant constructs a building to his specifications then sells the structure to developers and then leases it back at an agreed price. (The developers make a profit; the occupant has a building built to his specifications without tying up his working capital.)

SALES TAX. A tax on money received from the sale of goods, and, in some cases, services.

SALIC ROCKS. (1) Feldspar, quartz, etc. (2) Igneous rocks consisting primarily of silica and alumina.

SALIENT. (1) Prominent; conspicuous, important; cogent. (2) The part of a fortification or trench that protrudes toward the enemy.

SALINE. Salty; containing salt.

SALTBOX. A small, two-story house of square plan having a gable roof with the steeper and shorter pitch at the front of the house.

SALT LICK. A salt spring or dried salt pond.

SALT MARSH. Low coastal land frequently overflowed by the tide.

SALT MEADOW. A salt marsh covered with coarse grass.

SALVAGE. Anything saved from distruction; recovered items.

SAMP. Coarse, hulled Indian corn.

SAMPLE THIEF. Apparatus for taking samples of preservatives from tanks and other containers.

SANATARIUM. An institution for treatment of invalids. Often confused with sanatorium.

SANATORIUM. A convalescent establishment, more of a recuperative resort than a sanatarium.

SANCUTARY. The part of a church where the altar is located.

SANDHOG. One who works under air pressure in a tunnel, caisson, etc.

SANDWICH LEASE. The sandwich, (prime lessee) receiving fixed income representing the difference between the rental paid the fee owner by the prime lessee and the subrental received by the prime lessee from the sublessee. This technique is sometimes referred to as the Hawaiian or pineapple technique, and was reputedly devised by William Zeckendorf, a real estate developer.

SANITARY DISTRICT. An area set aside by a governmental unit for purposes of waste disposal. Property owners in the area are usually required to connect with the sewer mains and are assessed for services.

SANITARY LANDFILL. An area set aside for the dumping of trash and covered by layers of earth.

SAPONIFY. To convert fat into soap by action of an alkali.

SAPWOOD. Outer layers of growth in a tree, exclusive of bark, which contains living elements lighter in color than the heartwood.

SASH. The framework on which panes of glass are set in a window.

SATELLITE INDUSTRY. A company, supplier or consumer, which has located in proximity to a manufacturing plant either using its products or which produces products which may be used by the industry near which the *satellite* has located.

SATISFACTION PIECE. An instrument for recording and acknowledging payment of an indebtedness secured by a mortgage.

SATISFICING. Lying somewhere between satisfaction and optimal perfection.

SATURATION POINT. Sales, services, and/or production have reached the *saturation point* when the optimum market has been satisfied and there are no longer customers or sales areas for the products.

SAW PIT. A pit over which timber is laid to be sawed by two sawyers, one of whom is standing in the pit.

SAWTOOTH CONSTRUCTION. A roof so constructed that there are a series of sawtooth-like windowed upright roof extensions for the express purpose of gaining the most daylight for the interior of the building. Because of modern, artificial lighting systems, this type construction, which was quite costly, is seldom used.

SBIC. (See *SMALL BUSINESS INVESTMENT COMPANY*) An SBIC is a privately-owned institution licensed by the Small Business Administration and although the SBIC must operate within SBA regulations, its transactions with small companies are private arrangements and have no direct connection with the SBA. An SBIC may be formed by any three (or more) parties, but it must be chartered by the state in which it is formed, and no individual bank can own more than 49 percent of any SBIC. Minimum initial private capitalization is $150,000. SBICs may lend or invest only a maximum of 20 percent of their initial private capital to any one borrowing company. After 75 percent of the initial private capital has been loaned out, the SBIC may then borrow additional capital from SBA at the rate of two dollars for each dollar loaned out.

SCALAR. A quantity having magnitude only as mass or volume.

SCALENE. A triangle with three unequal sides.

SCAPE. The shaft of a column or pillar.

SCAR. (1) A bare rock standing alone. (2) A cliff or rocky place in the side of a hill or mountain.

SCARF. In carpentry, a lapped joint made by notching two timbers at the ends and joining them so as to make one continuous piece.

SCARP. A steep, or abrupt, slope.

SCHEELITE. A vitreous multicolored calcium tungsten.

SCHEMA. (1) A scheme; synopsis; summary. (2) A diagram sketch of a process, organization, etc.

SCHIST. Any rock that easily splits or cleaves into parallel layers.

SCHOONER. A fore and aft rigged vessel having two or more masts.

SCONCE. (1) A protective shelter. (2) An ornamental wall bracket for holding a candle or other light.

SCORIA. Refuse or slag after metal has been melted.

SCOTIA. A concave molding.

SCOUR. (1) To thoroughly clean. (2) To undercut as action of a stream against its banks.

SCOW. A barge or flat-bottomed boat with square ends without power of its own.

SCREE. (1) The waste from a quarry operation. (2) A mass of rocky debris at the foot of an incline.

SCREW PILE. A piling with a metal base which has a screw thread, for use in bedrock or extremely hard ground.

SCRIP. (1) Substitute paper money. (2) A provisional document certifying that the holder is entitled to receive something else (such as a property).

SCUPPER. A gutter along the deck of a vessel to facilitate water runoff.

SCUTCH. To dress fibres by beating.

SEAL. (1) A metal or plastic closure put on railroad freight car doors to seal the contents from entry. (2) A stamp or seal of a governmental body attached to documents to verify authenticity.

SEA LAWYER. A sailor given to carping and criticizing.

SEA LEVEL. (1) The assumed mean level of the sea's surface. (2) The actual mean level of the sea's surface as determined at a specific point.

SEAM. A strata of rock or minerals; a vein.

SEASONAL EMPLOYMENT. Work available only at certain times of the year, such as canning of vegetables.

SECONDARY BOYCOTT. (1) A sympathy boycott. (2) A boycott on purchases of other products of a firm already under boycott for another product. (3) Pressure exerted by a union on a neutral party who in turn exerts pressure against the actual adversary company.

SECONDARY DISTRIBUTION SYSTEM. A low-voltage AC system which connects the secondaries of the distributer transformers to the customer's services.

SECOND MORTGAGE. A mortgage given next after and subordinate to a first mortgage; a second deed of trust.

SECTION. An area of land one mile square containing 640 acres and constituting 1/36 of a township.

SECTION GANG. A work crew assigned to a specific section of a railroad.

SECTOR. A part of a circle bounded by two radii and the arc which is subtended by the radii.

SECURITY AGREEMENT. A document in which property (other than real estate) is pledged as security on a loan.

SEED CAPITAL, SEED MONEY. Money invested in a new business to attract other investors.

SEGMENT. Portion; part.

SEINE. A long fish net supported by buoys with weights under water at the bottom to trap fish.

SEISM. An earthquake.

SELECTMAN. In New England, an annually elected member of the Town Board.

SEMINAR. A group meeting to discuss mutual problems; a meeting of a group to hear lectures and discussions relating to the main interests of the group.

SEMISKILLED. Partially skilled workers not well enough trained or educated to perform specialized work.

SEMITRAILER. A truck equipped with one or more axles and so constructed that the front end rests upon the "fifth wheel" of a truck tractor; a semi.

SEPTIC TANK. A tank in which sewage drains and is allowed to remain until purified by chemical action.

SERIES WINDING. The winding of a dynamo or motor so that the field of current is connected in series with the armature circuit.

SERPENTINE WALL. A wall built in a winding and meandering manner so that it resembles the trail of a serpent. (An excellent example may be observed in the campus area of the University of Virginia at Charlottesville. That wall was designed by Thomas Jefferson.)

SERVICE INDUSTRY. An industry or firm furnishing services rather than producing manufactured goods; a maintenance firm, etc..

SETBACK. The distance from the street curb to the building facade. *Minimal setbacks* are required in planned industrial parks. Also, zoning regulations elsewhere may require such.

SETTLEMENT. The conveyance of property.

SEVERALTY. The holding of land in one's own right without participation; sole ownership or tenancy.

SEWAGE. Waste matter.

SEWERAGE. A sewer system.

SFERICS. An electronic device for the detection of electrical discharges in the atmosphere.

SHAFT. (1) A vertical or inclined excavation in mining operations. (2) Tunnel of a blast furnance. (3) Vertical opening through a building for the passage of elevators.

SHALE. An argillaceous rock with uneven laminations resembling slate.

SHALE OIL. Petroleum obtained by distillation of bituminous shales.

SHARD. A pottery fragment.

SHARE. (1) Interest owned by one of a number. (2) Unit of stock.

SHEEP'S-FOOT. A road roller with raised spurs for breaking up dirt, etc., in the preparation of a highway roadbed.

SHEET PILES. Piles driven in close contact in order to provide a tight wall so as to prevent leakage and/or to resist the pressure of adjacent ground.

SHELF. (1) A projecting ledge, as of rock. (2) A reef; shoal. (3) Stratum of bed rock encountered in sinking a shaft or in a test boring.

SHELL BUILDING. A building unfinished as to interior, usually built on speculation, to be finished to a client's specifications. Usually consists of only walls and roof.

SHIFT ANALYSIS AND INDUSTRIAL MIX. An analysis to determine the "standing" of manufacturing operations in a particular area versus the nation as a whole. (This is explained in more detail in the Handbook section.)

SHIM. (1) A wedge. (2) A small piece of wood or metal placed between two members of a structure for the purpose of leveling or bringing the members to a desired relative elevation.

SHINPLASTER. Currency or scrip used by private companies.

SHIPPING ORDER. Instructions to a carrier for transportation of cargo. Usually a copy of the Bill of Lading.

SHIP TRAIN. A train scheduled to connect with a ship; a boat train.

SHOAL. A shallow place in a body of water; a sand bar.

SHOPPING CENTER. A group of retail stores and service establishments comprising an architectural complex including large areas for parking.

SHORING. Strengthening; propping.

SHORT-TERM CAPITAL GAIN. A capital gain realized in less than six months and taxed in the same manner and rate as personal income.

SHORT-TERM DEBT. Indebtedness payable on demand or which is payable within one year from the date of issuance.

SHOTCRETE. A material consisting of Portland Cement, sand, and water projected on a surface pneumatically.

SHRINKAGE. Depreciation; decrease in value; undetermined loss.

SHUNT. (1) A by-pass. (2) An electric conductor joining two points in a circuit and serving to divert part of the current to an auxiliary circuit.

SHUTDOWN. The closing or ceasing of work in a mine, factory, or other operation.

SHUTOUT. A lockout.

SIC. Standard Industrial Classification.

SIDETRACK. An extension of a railroad track, including switch connection, from an industrial track to serve one customer exclusively.

SIDING. A railroad track by the side of and parallel to the main track used by slow-moving trains to allow express and faster trains to pass; also sometimes used for the storage of railroad cars.

SIERRA. A mountain range, especially one with a rugged outline.

SIGHT DRAFT. A bill or draft payable upon presentation.

SILEX. (Trademark.) Glass that is resistant to high temperatures; Pyrex.

SILICEOUS. Relating to or derived from silica.

SILO. (1) A cylindrical tower used for storage of materials. (2) An underground structure for the storage and launching of rockets. (3) An above ground structure in the launching area for space rockets, manned and unmanned.

SILVICULTURE. The production and tending a forest and its trees.

SIMPLE LISTING. An open listing of real estate with a broker but without an exclusive right-to-sell contract.

SIMULCAST. Broadcast by radio and television simultaneously.

SINE DIE. Without day; indefinitely.

SINE PROLE. Without offspring.

SINE QUA NON. (1) Without which none (nothing.) (2) An essential thing.

SINGLE PHASE. Designating an AC current having one phase at any given instant.

SINGLE TREE. The pivotal swinging bar to which the traces of a harness are fastened and by which the vehicle is drawn by one animal.

SINKHOLE. A natural cavity, especially a drainage cavity, as a hole worn through a rock along a joint or fracture.

SINKING FUND. Assets set apart for retirement of debt, redemption of stock or bonds, or for the protection of an investment in depreciable property.

SINTER. To make metal particles cohesive by the combined action of heat and pressure.

SIT-DOWN. A strike during which the strikers refuse to leave their place of employment until some agreement is reached with management.

SITE. A plot of ground set aside for a specific purpose or offered as such.

SKELETONIZE. To reduce in size or number.

SKELP. A strip of iron or steel from which tubes are produced.

SKEW ANGLE. An angle having an axis of any angle except a right angle.

SKIFF. A light row boat or small open sailing vessel light enough to be rowed with ease.

SKILLED LABOR. Workers capable of performing specialized work with a minimum of supervision and/or instruction.

SKYLEASE. (1) Lease for a long period a space above a piece of real estate. (2) Upper stories of a building to be erected by a tenant and become the property of the lessor at the termination of the lease.

SLAG. A nonmetallic fused product resulting from the reduction of ores in a furnace.

SLAKE. (1) To mix with water. (2) To become disintegrated and hydrated, as lime.

SLANDER. An oral statement of a false, malicious, or defamatory nature tending to damage another's reputation. Subject to suit.

SLEDGE. (1) A vehicle on runners for moving loads from one area to another. (2) A heavy hammer.

SLEEPER. (1) A railroad sleeping car. (2) A heavy beam resting on, or in, the ground as a support for a roadway, rails, etc.

SLIDING SCALE. A schedule affecting imports, prices, or wages under varying conditions of consumption, demand, or markets.

SLIT TRENCH. A narrow ditch.

SLOOP. A single-masted fore-and-aft-rigged sailing vessel carrying at least one jib.

SLOUGH. (1) A bog area. (2) An arroto. (3) A stagnate backwater.

SLOWDOWN. A slackening pace of production by either workers or management.

SLUDGE. Sediment.

SLUE. A slough.

SLUICE GATES. Gates built into the masonry of reservoirs or dams.

SLUMP. The shortening of a standard test mass of freshly-mixe concrete used as a measure of consistency.

SMALL BUSINESS. The U.S. Small Business Administration defines small business in these categories; *Manufacturing*—The operation is considered "small" if average employment in the preceding four quarters did not exceed 250 workers; "large" if average employment exceeded 1,000. If employment was between 250 and 1,000 SBA bases its determination on a specific size pattern for that particular industrial classification. *Wholesaling*—"Small" if annual sales do not exceed $5 million. *Retailing and Service*—"Small" if sales and receipts are not over $1 million.

SMALL BUSINESS ADMINISTRATION (SBA). An agency of the United States government established for the express purpose of assisting small businesses with financial and technical support.

SMALL BUSINESS INVESTMENT COMPANY (SBIC). An SBIC is a privately-owned institution licensed by SBA. Although an SBIC must operate within SBA regulations, their transactions with small companies are private arrangements and have no direct connection with SBA. An

SBIC may be formed by any three (or more) parties, but must be chartered in the state in which it is formed, and no individual bank can own more than 49 percent of any SBIC. Minimum initial private capitalization is $150,000. SBICs may lend or invest only a maximum of 20 percent of their initial private capital to any one borrowing company. After 75 percent of the initial private capital has been loaned out, the SBIC may then borrow additional capital from SBA at the rate of two dollars for each dollar loaned out. Parties interested in forming an SBIC should contact their SBA regional office to obtain details and official guidance.

SMELTER. A furnace for fusing ores in a reduction process to produce metal.

SNOW FENCE. A portable, slatted, lightweight fencing used to prevent snow drifting over roadways by causing it to drift elsewhere.

SNOW LINE. The limits of perpetual snow on the sides of mountains.

SNYE. A side channel in a river or other stream.

SOAKING PIT. A vertical reheating furnace in which ingots, after being stripped, are placed in an upright position for the purpose of uniformly reheating them to the temperature required for rolling.

SOCIAL CONTRACT. The theory that society evolved from association of individuals for their mutual protection and that the surrender of individual sovereignty was made through mutual consent rather than force.

SOCLE. (1) A square block higher than a plinth supporting a statue. (2) A base-supporting wall.

SODA ASH. An anhydrous sodium carbonate used in glassmaking.

SOFFIT. The underside of a beam or other projection.

SOFTWOOD. One of the group of trees which have needle-like leaves. The term has no reference to the softness of the wood.

SOIL PIPE. A pipe used for the drainage of an area, particularly underground drainage.

SOLID WASTE. Trash; litter other than sewage.

SOLVAY PROCESS. A method of making soda by passing carbon dioxide through a concentrated solution of common salt saturated with ammonia yielding sodium bicarbonate that is converted into soda by heating.

SOLVENCY. The condition of being able to meet all bills, debts, and obligations and having more assets than liabilities.

SPACE HEATER. A unit designed to heat a specific area.

SPACKLE. A plaster-like powder mixed to form a paste used for filling cracks and blemishes in walls, ceilings, etc., before painting.

SPANDREL. The portion of a structure above the extrados of an arch.

SPEAR. The paternal or male side of the family.

SPECIAL USE. A designated use which may be permitted in a differently zoned district upon approval of the municipality or an appointed board with such power.

SPECIAL WARRENTY DEED. (1) Limited warrenty. (2) A deed wherein the grantor limits his liability to the grantee.

SPECIFICATION. A written description and enumeration of particulars.

SPECIFIC GRAVITY. (1) The ratio of the mass of a body to that of an equal volume of some standard substance: water, in the case of liquids; air or hydrogen, in the case of gases. (2) A measure of density.

SPECIFIC HEAT. The amount of heat required to raise the temperature of one gram of a given substance one degree centigrade measured in calories.

SPECIFIC PERFORMANCE. A court of equity ruling compelling a party to carry out all the terms of a contract or agreement.

SPECULATIVE BUILDING. A building erected without a tenant or buyer in the hope that it will be purchased by an employer-user in the future. Such buildings are rarely in a completely finished state; usually only the walls and roof are completed so that a building may be finished to the specifications of the occupant

SPILLWAY. A low-level. passage serving a dam or reservoir through which surplus water may be discharged.

SPOLIATION. Destruction, mutilation, or alteration of an instrument such as a will, deed, bill of exchange, etc.

SPOT ZONING. A zoning status accorded a property different than that prevailing in the surrounding or immediate area.

SPRAG. (1) A wooden prop to support a roof of ore in a mine; a mine prop. (2) A chock or steel bar used to prevent the slippage or roll-back of a vehicle on an incline.

SPREAD. (1) An acreage. (2) A colloquialism defining a farm or ranch area.

SPREAD FOOTERS. Foundation piling used to maintain stability and give additional strength in a spongy or soft soil.

SPRINKLER SYSTEM. A device for stemming fires through an arrangement of pipes in the ceilings of a building with outlets which sprinkle water automatically when a predetermined temperature is reached.

SPUR. An extension of railroad track (including switch connection) from an industrial track to serve two or more users.

SQUARE FOOT. One foot square.

SQUARE FOOTAGE. Measurement of the number of square feet comprising an area.

STADIA. (1) A temporary surveying station. (2) A graduated stick held at arm's length as a simple aid in measuring short distances.

STAIRWELL. A vertical shaft enclosing a staircase.

STALACTITE. A long tapering formation hanging from the ceiling of a cavern produced by continuous watery deposits containing certain minerals.

STALAGMITE. An incrustation on the floor (ground) of a cavern built up into conical shape by drippings of minerals from above.

STAMP MILL. A machine for pulverizing rock for the purpose of extracting the ore it contains.

STAMPING MILL. A machine or operation where metal stampings are formed.

STANDARD CANDLE. A unit of luminous intensity equal to that of 1/60 square centimeter of a black body operating at the temperature of solidification of platinum.

STANDARD GAUGE. (1) A gauge for determining whether tools are of standard size. (2) A railroad track width of 56½ inches.

STANDARD INDUSTRIAL CLASSIFICATION (SIC). Numbered classification by the U.S. government Bureau of the Census designating establishments by type of product or industrial activity.

STANDARD METROPOLITAN AREA (SMA) A central area of 50,000 population or more plus the surrounding counties from which at least 15 percent normally commute to the urban area for employment.

STANDARD METROPOLITAN STATISTICAL AREA (SMSA). Basically the same as the standard metropolitan area (with some exceptions) upon which statistical analysis is based and correlated.

STANDPIPE. A vertical pipe for the storage of water; a water tower.

STANNARY. A tin mine or region of tin mines.

STANNIC. Containing tin.

STANNUM. Tin.

STARBOARD. The right side of a boat as one faces forward.

STATE BANK. (1) A bank that has a charter from a state government. (2) Any bank that is owned or controlled by a state.

STATE UNIVERSITY. An institution of learning maintained in and supported by a state and considered a part of the state educational system.

STATOR. The stationary portion of a dynamo, tubine, motor, etc.

STATUTE. A law; legal ordinance.

STEAMFITTER. A person who sets up or repairs steam pipes and their fittings.

STEAM POINT. The boiling point of water (100°C.; 212°F.)

STEELYARD. A weighing device of a scaled beam counterpoise and hooks. (The article to be weighed is hung at the short end and the counterpoise weight on the long arm.)

STEEPLEJACK. A person whose occupation is to inspect, renovate, or repair tall structures such as church steeples, industrial chimneys, standpipes, and the like.

STEERAGEWAY. The lowest speed at which a vessel may be steered accurately and with control.

STELE, STELA. An upright sculptured slab or tablet of stone.

STEP DOWN. The conversion of high voltage into lower voltage.

STEP UP. The conversion of low voltage into higher voltage.

STERE. A metric measure of capacity equal to one cubic meter.

STILE. (1) A series of steps on either side of a fence or wall. (2) One of the vertical side pieces in a door or window sash.

STILT. A tall post or pillar used as support or underpinning of a dock or building.

STIPULATE. (1) To specify, as terms of a contract, etc. (2) To promise; guarantee.

STITHY. (1) An anvil. (2) A smithy or forge.

STOA. A covered colonnade.

STOB. A stake or post or a stump of a tree.

STOCHASTIC. Conjectural.

STOCKADE. A line of stout posts set straight upright in the earth to form a fence or barrier.

STOCK CERTIFICATE. A document testifying to investment in the issuing company.

STOCK FARM. A farm specializing in the breeding of livestock.

STOCK GUARD. A barrier placed between and alongside a railroad track to prevent the passage of livestock on or along the tracks.

STOCKPASS. A culvert of bridge opening under or above a railroad track primarily for the passage of livestock from one field to another.

STOKEHOLD. The furnace room of a ship.

STOKEHOLE. The space about the mouth of a furnace or the mouth itself.

STOKER. A person or device for feeding fuel to the furnance.

STOL. Short take-off and landing airoraft.

STONEMASON. One whose occupation is to prepare and place construction stones.

STONEWARE. A variety of very hard pottery made from siliceous clay or clay mixed with flint and sand. The product is impervious to heat and cold and, in dinnerware, may be moved directly from icebox or freezer to preheated oven without damage.

STOOP. A small porch at the entrance to a house.

STOPE. An excavation from which the ore is removed either above or below a certain level in a series of steps; strip mining.

STOP-OFF; STOPOVER. A privilege on carload shipments at stations between points of origin and final destination, for the purposes of finishing loading or partly unloading, or taking advantage of transit or other privileges. A special charge is usually made in addition to normal transportation service rates.

STOPPAGE. (1) Halting of plant operations for any reason, especially. *work stoppage*. (2) A deduction from pay to repay something (not a garnishment).

STORAGE BATTERY. A direct current battery capable of being recharged.

STORAGE-IN-TRANSIT. A tariff provision under which a shipper is allowed to stop his shipment for temporary storage at a point intermediate to origin and destination without penalty.

STOSS. Facing the direction in which a glacier moves; said of a hill.

STRAIGHT TRUCK. A truck with the body and engine mounted on the same chassis, as differentiated from a "semi."

STRAKE. A continous band of hull planking on a vessel.

STRAND. The portion of an ocean beach between low and high tides.

STRATIFIED. Arranged in layers.

STRATOSPHERE. (1) Isothermal layer. (2) The portion of the atmosphere beginning at a height of about seven miles and characterized by a relatively uniform temperature.

STRATUM. A layer, bed, or thickness as in rock formations (plural—strata).

STRAWBOARD. A coarse board made of pressed straw and used for boxes and book covers.

STREAM FLOW. The quantity of water passing a given point in a stream in a given period of time. Usually expressed in cubic feet per second.

STRIA. A small groove or ridge in a rock surface due to action of glacier ice.

STRINGCOURSE. A horizontal molding or ornamental brick or stone projecting along the face of a building.

STRINGER. A longitudinal member extending from bent to bent.

STRIP MINING. Surface mining.

STRIP ZONING. Zoning of areas in narrow strips usually fronting on a main highway or street for commercial purposes.

STRUCK JURY. A process by which each party strikes twelve names from a list of forty-eight. The remaining twenty-four constitute the panel from which the final jury of twelve is chosen.

STRUCTURAL IRON. (1) Iron adapted for use in construction. (2) Iron formed into special shapes for construction purposes.

STRUCTURAL STEEL. Steel prepared for use in building construction.

STRUT. A part of a framework designed to relieve weight or strain in the direction of its length.

STUCCO. A firm plaster made of Portland cement, sand, and lime, used mostly for wall coatings, both inside and outside.

STUD. (1) A short intermediate post as in a building frame. (2) A post to which laths and wallboard are fastened.

STUDDING. Studs or joists, collectively.

SUBASSEMBLY. An assembled part that is, in turn, part of a larger assembly.

SUBCONTRACT. A contract subordinate to another contract and assigning part of the work to another party.

SUBDIVISION. An area divided into lots for sale for housing, or the area in which the houses are located or are to be built.

SUBDRAIN. A covered drain below ground-surface receiving water along its length through perforations, grilles, or joints.

SUBFLOOR. The rough flooring upon which a finished floor is laid.

SUBJACENT. (1) Situated directly beneath. (2) Lower, but *not* directly below.

SUBLEASE. A lease of property from a primary tenant to another.

SUBLETTING. A leasing by one tenant to a subtenant.

SUBLITERAL. (1) Close to the seashore. (2) Designating the area between low tide mark and a depth of twenty fathoms.

SUBMARGINAL. (1) Below margin. (2) Land of low fertility, underproduction, or unsatisfactory use potential.

SUBORDINATE. (1) Lower; minor; secondary. (2) Subject or secondary to another, as in making one creditor subordinate to a more preferred creditor because of prior claim.

SUBORN. To perjure; bribe.

SUBPOENA. (1) A judicial summons requiring a person to appear in court. (2) A judicial writ requiring certain papers to be presented to a court or trial.

SUBREGION. A subdivision of a region, as a development district.

SUBROGATION. (1) Putting one thing in place of another. (2) Substitution of one creditor for another.

SUB ROSA. Confidential; secret.

SUBSIDENCE. A gradual settling of earth because of ground movements caused sometimes by undergound mine workings, erosion, etc.

SUBSIDY. Pecunious aid granted by a government to an enterprise deemed of benefit to the general public.

SUBSOIL. The stratum of earth next beneath the surface soil.

SUBSTANDARD. Inferior to an established norm or acceptable standard.

SUBSTANTIVE. Independent in resources.

SUBSTRATUM. (1) An underlying layer. (2) Subsoil.

SUBSTRUCTURE. (1) A structure serving as a foundation of a building. (2) The earthen roadbed supporting railroad tracks or paved highway.

SUBSURFACE DRAINAGE. The control and removal of excess moisture contained in the soil.

SUBURBIA. The area, usually residential with shopping areas, next to or near a large urban area; the outskirts and outlying districts of a municipality.

SUCTION PUMP. A pump operating by suction, consisting of a piston working on a cylinder both of which are equipped with valves.

SUITE. A number of connected rooms.

SULCUS. A narrow channel or furrow.

SUMMONS. A citation to appear in court or before a judge, magistrate, or referee.

SUMP. (1) A depression at the lowest level of a mine shaft. (2) A cesspool or reservoir for drainage.

SUNK FENCE. (1) A ditch having a retaining wall on one side to divide lands or land ownership. (2) A ha-ha.

SUPERANNUATED. (1) Retired on account of age. (2) Obsolete; outdated.

SUPERHIGHWAY. A road for high-speed traffic with four or more lanes divided by a safety median or wall between cars and other traffic moving in opposite directions.

SUPERPOSE. Lying over or upon something else, as one layer upon another.

SUPPORTING WALL. A wall which is an integral part of a building and lends support to floors above.

SURBASE. A molding or border above the base of a pedestal or baseborad.

SURETY. (1) Pledge or guarantee; security. (2) Sponsor.

SURPLUS PROPERTY. Surplus property is material or real estate which the General Services Administration of the U.S. government determines is not needed by the federal government and which may be donated to educational, public health, and civil defense organizations; public airports, educational activities of special interest to the armed services; the American Red Cross and public bodies. Property and materiel not wanted by any of the foregoing may be offered to the general public by the General Services Administration.

SURRENDER. The cancellation of a lease by mutual consent.

SURROGATE. (1) Substitute. (2) Probate judge. (3) One who is put in the place of another.

SURTAX. An additional tax, such as a graduated income tax, over and above a fixed income tax.

SURVEY. (1) A study. (2) Inspection and measurement by instruments.

SUSPEND. (1) To fail. (2) To desist. (3) To stop payment.

SUSPENSE ACCOUNT. An account in which charges or credits are entered temporarily pending determination of their proper depositor.

SUSPENSION BRIDGE. A bridge on which the roadway is hung from cables strongly anchored over towers and without intervening support from below.

SUSTAINED GRADE. A continuous highway grade of appreciable length and of consistent gradient.

SWAMP. A place where the water table is at ground level; a bog.

SWARD. Land thickly covered with grass; turf.

SWITCHBACK. A railroad or highway ascending an incline in a zigzag pattern in order to reduce the rate of climb or descent.

SWITCHING LIMITS. The extent of the area within which railroad cars may be moved under *switching rates*.

SWITCHYARD. A railroad yard for the assembling and breaking up of trains into proper classifications.

SYLVAN. Wooded.

SYMPATHY STRIKE. A secondary strike by a union not directly involved with the prime work stoppage. (A transportation union may refuse to serve a firm struck by its operating union.)

SYMPOSIUM. (1) A meeting for discussion of a particular subject. (2) A series of articles on the same or similar subjects.

SYNCLINE. A system of stratified rock in which the strata incline upward on each side from the axis of the fold.

SYNDICATE. An association of individuals joined together to negotiate some business or to prosecute some enterprise requiring a large amount of capital.

SYNERGY. Combined and united actions.

SYPHER. To make a lap joint.

T

TABLELAND. A plateau; a broad and level elevated area.

TACE, TASSE. A type of armor plate.

TACHOGRAPH. A device in the cab of a truck to automatically record mileage, number of stops, speed, and other factors during a trip.

TACONITE. An inferior iron ore found in the Mesabi district of Minnesota.

TAFFRAIL. The rail around a vessel's stern.

TAILING. (1) Refuse or residue from grain after milling or from ground ore after washing. (2) The inner, covered portion of a projecting brick or stone in a wall.

TALC. A soft, hydrous silicate used in making paper, soap, talcum powder, etc.

TALESMAN. One who is summoned for jury duty after the regular panel has been exhausted by challenges.

TALUS SLOPE. (1) A slope formed by an accumulation of rock debris. (2) Rock debris, as at the base of a cliff.

TAN. To convert into leather by treating hides with tannin.

TANGENT. (1) A straight line in contact with a curve at one point. (2) Any straight portion of a railway alignment.

TANK CAR. A railroad car especially designed for hauling liquids.

TANKER. A cargo vessel, railroad tank car, or truck designed for transporting liquid cargo.

TANK FARM. An area occupied by large tanks, as at a petroleum distribution point or refinery storage area.

TANK TRUCK. A motor truck designed for hauling liquids.

TANNIN. A brownish-white astringent compound extracted from nuts, sumac, etc., used in the preparation of inks and the tanning of leather.

TAPPET. A projecting arm or lever that moves intermittently by automatically touching another part of a mechanism.

TAPPING. The removal of the molten metal from an open hearth furnace by opening the tap hole and allowing the metal to run into the ladle.

TARE. An allowance made by deducting the weight of a container from the gross weight of the container and its contents.

TARGET DATE. An agreed upon date at which time a contract or action is to be started or completed.

TARIFF. A schedule containing matter related to transportation movements, rates, rules and regulations.

TARN. A small mountain lake.

TASK FORCE. A tactical unit assigned to a specific task.

TAW. To convert leather by use of alum and salt rather than by tanning.

TAX ASSESSMENT. The official determination of the share a taxpayer within a taxing district must pay.

TAXIWAY. A supporting runway or apron for storing and moving aircraft to and from hangars and airport runways for flight.

T-BAR. An iron structural member in the shape of a "T" in profile.

T-BAR LIFT. A ski lift.

TEAM TRACK. A railroad track on which cars are placed for transfer of freight between railroad cars and highway vehicles.

TECHNICAL ASSISTANCE. Aid rendered to a person or group in the form of advice from experts in the fields of interest.

TECHNOCRACY. A theory that advocates control by an organized body of experts.

TECTONICS. The science or art of construction of large structures.

TEEMING. The pouring of molten steel from the ladle into ingot molds.

TEGULAR. Pertaining to, or resembling, tiles.

TEMPER. To bring metal to a required hardness and elasticity by heating and then suddenly cooling.

TEMPLATE. (1) A pattern or gauge used as a guide in shaping something accurately. (2) A stout stone or timber in a building for the purpose of distributing weight. (3) A wedge for a building block under a ship's keel.

TENANCY AT WILL. A license to use or occupy a property at the will of the owner.

TENANCY IN COMMON. An estate held by two or more persons, each of whom is considered as being possessed of the whole or an undivided part.

TENANT. (1) Lessee. (2) Occupant or dweller.

TENANT AT SUFFERANCE. One who comes into possession of lands by lawful title and retains it afterward with no title at all.

TENANT FARMER. (1) One who farms land owned by another and pays rent, usually in the form of crops or sharecropping. (2) One who lives on an owner-occupied farm and works for the landowner at stipulated wages. Housing, firewood, utilities and farm-grown food are usually fringe benefits accruing to the tenant farmer.

TENET. A principle; credo; belief.

TENON. A projection on the end of a timber for inserting into a socket to form a joint.

TENSILE. Capable of being drawn out.

TENSILE STRENGTH. The resistance of material to forces of rupture and stress, usually expressed in pounds per square inch.

TENURE. (1) A holding, such as land. (2) Term of office.

TERM. (1) A length of time; (2) Length of a note.

TERMINAL. (1) An assemblage of a facilities at a *railroad terminal* or at intermediate points for the purpose of assembling, breaking up, or relaying trains. (2) A point at which an electric circuit element may be connected to other elements. (3) A frieze or pedestal situated at the end of something.

TERMINAL VELOCITY. The speed acquired by a freely falling body when the resistance of the medium equals the gravitational forces acting upon the body.

TERMINUS. The end of the line of a railroad; road end.

TERM LOAN. A loan that matures after one to ten years and usually is paid in installments.

TERNE PLATE. Steel plate with a coating of lead and tin.

TERRACE. An artificially raised level space.

TERRA-COTTA. A hard, kiln-burnt clay, brick-colored and unglazed—used as a structural material.

TERRAIN. The nature of a tract of ground as to its topography.

TERRE TENANT. One who has actual possession of the land.

TERRITORIAL WATERS. Costal and inland waters under the jurisdiction of a state or nation.

TERTIAN. Occurring every other day, or every third day.

TERTIARY. Third in point of time, numbers, etc.

TESTACY. The state of having left a will.

TESTATOR. One who has left a will.

THALWEG. The line following the deepest part of the bed of a channel or stream.

THEODOLITE. An instrument for measuring horizontal and vertical angles by means of a small telescope turning on horizontal and vertical axes.

THEOREM. (1) An axiom. (2) A proposition demonstrably true or acknowledged as such.

THERM. A unit of heat equal to 100,000 BTUs.

THIRD RAIL. A rail that supplies current to the trains of an electric railroad.

THORP. A village.

THREE-MILE LIMIT. Internationally recognized territorial jurisdiction off the coasts of the nations throughout the world.

THREE-PHASE POWER. Designed for AC current of three branches differing by one-third of a cycle (120°) in phase so that when one branch is at full value the others are at half value but flowing in the opposite direction. This power is generally required for operating heavy equipment (see Handbook section).

THRESHOLD. (1) The doorway or sill. (2) The plank or stone lying under the door or doorway of a building.

THROUGHWAY, THRUWAY. A long-distance, high-speed limited access highway.

TIDELAND. An area alternately covered and uncovered by tides.

TIDERIP. A riptide; undertow.

TIDEWAITER. A customs officer who boards vessels entering a port to enforce regulations. (So-called because in early days, vessels waited for a suitable tide before entering a harbor.)

TIDEWATER. (1) Water that inundates land at high tide. (2) Any area, as a seacoast, whose waters are affected by the tides.

TIDEWATER VIRGINIA. The western shore of Virginia fronting on Chesapeake Bay.

TIE PLATE. A plate interposed between a rail and a railroad tie.

TILL. (1) Unstratified glacial drift consisting of clay, sand, gravel, and boulders intermingled. (2) A cash drawer.

TIMBER. (1) Wood suitable for structural purposes. (2) Standing trees; woodlands.

TIMBERLINE. The upper limit of tree growth on a hillside or mountain beyond which no trees can grow.

TIME AND MOTION STUDY. The analysis of movement involved in the performance of given repetitive tasks in order to find more efficient methods of performing the same operation; a time study.

TIME DEPOSIT. A bank deposit that cannot be withdrawn prior to a specified future time.

TINPLATE. Sheet metal plated with tin.

TIPPLE. (1) An apparatus for tipping loaded freight railroad cars for rapid unloading. (2) An apparatus at a coal mine for loading freight cars and trucks.

TITHE. A tax or assessment of one-tenth.

TITLE. (1) The means whereby the owner has just taken possession of property. (2) Legal evidence of the right of possession.

TITLE BY ADVERSE POSSESSION. Acquired by occupation and recognized as against the paper title owner; squatter's rights.

TITLE INSURANCE. A policy guaranteeing clear title to property. In the event transfer of title cannot be made due to lack of clear title, the buyer is recompensed for all damages by the insuror.

TITLE SEARCH. An investigation of all avenues to determine the title of a property.

TNT. Trinitrotoluene; an explosive.

TOE OF SLOPE. The intersection of a slope with the ground surface.

TOGGLE JOINT. A joint having a central hinge like an elbow and operable by applying power at the junction, thus changing the direction of force and giving mechanical pressure.

TOGGLE SWITCH. An electric switch in the form of a projecting lever whose movement through a small arc opens or closes an electric circuit.

TOKEN MONEY. (1) Earnest money. (2) Option money.

TON. (1) A short, or *net ton* = 2,000 pounds; a long, or *gross ton* = 2,240 pounds. (2) A unit for reckoning the weight of vessels. Thirty-five cubic feet of sea water weighs about one long ton; a displacement ton. (3) A unit for reckoning the freight-carrying capacity of a ship equivalent to forty cubic feet of space but varying with type of cargo.

TONGUE AND GROOVE. A projecting edge or tenon of a board for insertion into a corresponding groove of another board.

TON-MILE. Movement of one ton for a distance of one mile.

TONNAGE. The cubic capacity of a merchant vessel expressed in tons of 100 cubic feet each.

TONTINE. A form of collective life insurance by which the individual profits increase as the number of survivors diminish, the final survivor taking the whole.

TOPOGRAPHY. (1) Detailed description of an area with particular reference to grade contours. (2) The contour and other physical features of an area.

TOPONYM. The name of a place; any other name derived from the name of a place.

TOPSOIL. The surface layer; overburden.

TOR. A high, rocky hill or jutting rock.

TORT. (1) Any private or civil wrong by act or omission for which civil suit may be brought. (2) Injustice.

TOWHEAD. A bar in the Mississippi River system covered with vegetation or grassy growth.

TOWN. A community larger than a hamlet or village but not incorporated as a city.

TOWNHOUSE. A home built with adjoining houses usually with common walls and consisting of two or more floors.

TOWNSHIP. (1) A subdivision of a county with certain corporate powers of municipal government. (2) A unit of area in surveys of public lands, usually six miles square subdivided into 36 sections of one square mile each.

TOWPATH. A path along a river or canal used by draft animals or towing boats.

TRACE. A route; path.

TRACK. The railroad rails, ties and ballast (A width of 56½ inches).

TRACKAGE. (1) Railroad tracks, collectively. (2) The mileage of a railroad or section thereof. (3) *Trackage rights* permit one railroad company to use the tracks of another railroad company.

TRACK, BAD ORDER. A railroad track on which railroad cars in need of repair are placed.

TRACT. (1) Acreage. (2) A development. (3) An extended area as of land or water.

TRACTILE. Capable of being drawn out; ductile.

TRACTION ENGINE. A locomotive for hauling on ground as distinguished from one used on railroad tracks.

TRACTOR. (1) A motor-driven vehicle with cab used to haul trailers and semis. (2) A piece of motorized equipment for towing or for farm tilling.

TRADE DISCOUNT. A reduction from the list price given by a manufacturer or wholesaler to a buyer in the same trade.

TRADE OFF. The interaction between related activities such as the offsetting of high costs in one category by lower costs in another (e.g., transportation time versus cost of slower movement).

TRADE SCHOOL. A vocational school.

TRADE UNION. A labor union, usually a craft union.

TRAIL. A trace or path; a footpath.

TRAILER. (1) A vehicle drawn by a motorized piece of equipment. (2) A short motion picture used in advertising.

TRAILER COURT, TRAILER PARK. A large area equipped with sanitary facilities and utilities and having accommodations for parking passenger trailers and recreational vehicles.

TRAILING-POINT SWITCH. A railroad switch, the points of which face away from approaching traffic.

TRAIN. (1) A series of rolls in a rolling mill connected together and driven by the same engine or motor. (2) A railroad unit consisting of motive power and a number of freight or passenger cars. (3) To educate or prepare for employment in a specific field.

TRAINEE. One who undergoes training or retraining.

TRAIN OIL. Whale oil.

TRAJECTORY. The path described by an object moving in space.

TRAMROAD. A road or railroad in a mine.

TRANSACTION. A business deal.

TRANSFEREE. One to whom a transfer of property is made.

TRANSFEROR. One who excutes a transfer of property.

TRANSFER POINT. A station or stop at which freight is transferred from one railroad to another; from a railroad to truck; truck to truck; or truck to railroad. Also interchange from and to water carriers.

TRANSFER SLIP. A protected landing place for transfer boats to connect railroad tracks on land with those on the vessel.

TRANSFER TRACK. A railroad track so located to facilitate the transfer of lading from one railroad car to another.

TRANSFORMER. A device for changing the ratio of current to voltage in an AC system while keeping power substantially constant.

TRANSIT. A surveying instrument for measuring horizontal and vertical angles.

TRANSIT PRIVILEGE. A privilege accorded shippers and receivers of freight whereby certain commodities stop at an intermediate point for storage or further processing before proceeding to final destination. Usually a special charge is added to the freight rate which is the through rate from orgin to destination on the final processed commodity.

TRANSMISSION LINES. (1) Electric power lines for transporting large amounts of power over great distances. (2) Pipelines for transporting petroleum products or natural gas.

TRANSOM. A small hinged window over a doorway.

TRANSSHIP. To transfer goods from one transfer line to another, particularly between rail and water carriers.

TRANSPIRATION. Vaporization of water from vegetable surfaces.

TRAP. (1) traprock; aggregates. (2) Rocks used in road building.

TRAP CAR. A railroad car for hauling ballast or trap rock.

TRAPEZIUM. A four-sided, plane figure of which two sides are parallel; a trapezoid.

TRAPROCK. Dark, fine-grained igneous rock.

TRAVELING CRANE. A hoisting apparatus which moves along tracks on a supporting framework.

TREASURY BILLS. Investment tender issued by the Federal Reserve Bank in amounts of $10,000 and maturing in 91 to 182 days.

TREASURY BONDS. Long-term notes with maturity dates of not less than seven years and up to twenty-five years.

TREASURY NOTES. Short-term notes maturing in less than seven years.

TREE FARM. (1) A tree plantation. (2) An area devoted to growing trees to replace timber-cutting of a forest. (3) A tree nursery.

TREPAN. A large, rock-boring tool.

TRESPASS. Any wrongful act accompanied by force, either acutal or implied, such as wrongful entry on another's land.

TRESTLE. (1) A beam or bar supported by four divergent legs for bearing platforms. (2) An open braced framework for supporting a railroad or highway bridge.

TRET. An allowance for waste as a result of transportation.

TRIAL BALANCE. In double-entry bookkeeping, a draft or statement of debit and credit balances of each ledger account.

TRIANGULATE. (1) Divide into triangles. (2) A method of determining a position by taking bearings on two fixed points of known distance apart and computing the position and/or area of the resultant triangle.

TRIBUTARY. A stream flowing into a larger body of water.

TRIFID. Divided into three parts or sections.

TRINITROTOLUENE (TNT). An explosive. Often erroneously referred to as dynamite, which has a nitroglycerin base.

TRIODE. A three-element electron tube containing an anode, a cathode, and a control grid.

TRIPARTITE. (1) threefold. (2) Pertaining to the three parties, as in a *tripartite agreement*.

TRIPHASE. Employing three phases, as an alternating current.

TRIPPET. A cam or projecting piece designed to strike some other piece at fixed intervals.

TROLLEY. (1) A streetcar or tram. (2) Mechanism of a traveling crane. (3) A metal wheel for making contact with overhead wires to bring electric current to a conveyance. (4) A single-pole pantograph.

TROMPE. An apparatus for supplying a blast of air to a forge by action of a column of water falling through a perforated pipe and thus carrying air by entanglement.

TRUE BILL. The endorsement by a grand jury on a bill of indictment that the jurors find to be sustained by the evidence.

TRUNDLE. (1) A roller caster. (2) A small, low-wheeled dolly.

TRUSS. A braced framework for support of a roof. (Inside height dimension of a building is usually referred to as so many feet clearance under truss.)

TRUST. A syndicate; a permanent combination formed for the purpose of controlling product, prices, etc., of some commodity or the management, profits, etc., of some business.

TRUST COMPANY. An incorporated institution formed to accept and execute trusts; to receive deposits of money and other personal property, issue obligations for them; and lend money.

TRUST DEED. A conveyance of real estate to a third person to be held for the benefit of a beneficiary.

TRUSTEE. (1) One who holds property in trust. (2) A member of a ruling board of directors.

TRUST FUND. Money, securities, etc., held in trust.

TUBULE. A minute or very small tube.

TULE. A large bullrush growing on damp or flooded land in the southwestern region of the United States.

TUN. (1) A large cask or vat. (2) A brewer's fermenting vat. (3) A measure of capacity equal to 252 gallons.

TUNGSTATE. A salt of tungstic acid.

TUNGSTEN. (1) Wolfram. (2) A heavy metal of the chrominum group occuring in scheelite and wolframite having a high melting point and much used in the production of filaments for electric lamps and high-speed cutting tools.

TUNGSTIC. Pertaining to or containing tungsten, especially in its higher proportions.

TURBID. (1) Opaque or cloudy (liquid) (2) Thick, dense (air.)

TURBIDITY. A measure of suspended matter in air of water.

TURGID. Unnaturally distended, as by contained air or liquid.

TURN-KEY JOB. A project completed according to detailed specifications and turned over to a tenant, owner, or other occupant mor use.

TURN-KEY PLANT. A package whereby an industry may be provided with land, bulding (and in some instances, equipment) with rental/lease covering all aspects. This type of arrangement is often offered prospects by local development corporations endeavoring to improve the economic climate of an area. Builders with sound financial backing may also contract to provide the complete "package" so as to permit a client to retain his working capital and other assets for use in operations of the plant.

TURNOUT. An arrangement of a railroad switch and a frog with closure rails, by means of which railroad rolling stock may be diverted from one track to another.

TUSCAN ORDER. A Roman order of arch resembling Roman Doric but having no decorated details.

TWO-PHASE. (1) Diphase. (2) Having two phases as two alternating currents, the maximum and minimum of which differ from one another by ninety degrees.

TYPOGRAPHY. The arrangement of composed type.

U

ULTIMO. In the last month.

UNDEREMPLOYED. (1) Employed in a job not up to the capabilities of the worker. (2) Working too few hours.

UNDERLEASE. A sublease.

UNDERPASS. A passage of a highway beneath a road or railroad.

UNDERPINNING. Material or framework used to support a structure from below.

UNDERSTRATUM. Substratum; underlying stratum.

UNDERWRITE. (1) To finance; subscribe. (2) To insure.

UNEARNED INCOME. Income received from rent, dividends, interest, etc., but not from wages or business operations.

UNEMPLOYABLE. A person, who, because of illness, mental deficiency, or physical handicap cannot work in any job.

UNILATERAL. (1) Single. (2) Action taken by only one party.

UNION SHOP. An establishment that hires only members of a labor union or those who agree to join such within a specified time; a closed shop.

UNION STATION. A train depot jointly operated by more than one railroad, or jointly served by more than one railroad.

UNITIZATION. The technique of consolidating several small shipments into a single unit.

UNSKILLED. (1) Menial or common. (2) Destitute of skills in any field except the most menial tasks.

UNTITLED. Having no right or claim.

UNWRITTEN LAW. A rule or custom established by general usage rather than by legal statute.

URBAN. Pertaining to a city.

URBAN RENEWAL. (1) The planned upgrading of a deteriorated or deteriorating urban area by using public funds and overseen by a government agency. (2) A In-city redevelopment.

USE. The specific purpose for which land or building is designated.

USURY. Charging more than the legal rate of interest allowed.

UTILITY COMPANY. A firm or agglomerate providing electric power, gas supply, water, or sewer service. Railroads are also usually included in this category by developers.

V

VACANT. (1) Empty; unused. (2) Unoccupied or unused, having neither claimant nor heir for an estate.

VALANCE. A short drapery board across the top of a window.

VALIDATE. Ratify; confirm.

VALUABLE CONSIDERATION. Something of value given to justify or confirm an action, as with the transfer of deed or property, etc.

VALUATION. Estimate or appraisal of the value of property.

VALUED POLICY. An insurance policy requiring an insurance company to pay the insured the full amount of his policy regardlesss of the actual value of the property insured if it is totally destroyed.

VANADIUM. A rare silver-white metallic element used in steel alloys to increase the tensile strength of the product.

VANADIUM STEEL. Steel containing 0.1 percent to 0.25 percent vanadium.

VANDALISM. The willful destruction of property.

VARIANCE. A departure from specific zoning to permit an operation not conforming to the zoning regulations. Such permission must be obtained from and granted by the Zoning Board of Appeals. It applies only to a specific piece of property and is granted only for modification of land development.

VARVE. A pair of layers of alternately finer and coarser silt or clay believed to be an annual cycle of deposits in a lake or other body of still water.

VECTOR. (1) A line representing a physical quantity that has magnitude and direction in space such as velocity and acceleration. (2) A *radius vector* is the straight line distance from a fixed origin point to any point in a curve.

VENDEE. The party to whom something is sold; the buyer.

VENDER, VENDOR. The seller.

VENEER. A coating or thin covering of the same or different material than the basic material.

VENTURE CAPITAL. (1) Money used to support new or unusual undertakings. (2) Speculative or risk investment capital.

VERTICAL INTEGRATION. (1) Start-to-finish production. (The production company controls the economic steps from production of raw materials to the retail sales.) (2) Control from raw material to finished product.

VESTED. That which has become a consummate right, as a *vested interest* in a pension fund.

VESTIBULE. (1) An antechamber between the outer door of a building and an anterior door leading to the interior. (2) An enclosed passageway between railroad passenger cars.

VESTIBULE SCHOOL. A preparatory school.

VIABLE. (1) Practical; practicable. (2) Capable of working, as a plan. (3) Having growth potential, as a community.

VIADUCT. (1) A bridge-like structure to carry traffic over a valley ravine or congested area such as a city. (2) A "skyway."

VIDELICIT. To wit; namely.

VILLA. A luxurious home in the country. (In Britain, a modest suburban residence.)

VILLAGE. (1) A collection of houses, etc., in a rural district smaller than a town but larger than a hamlet. (2) In some are areas, defined as a municipality smaller than a city and sometimes unincorporated.

VITREOUS. (1) Glassy. (2) Resembling glass, but made of clay and highly polished.

VITREOUS ELECTRICITY. Electricity generated by rubbing glass with silk —regarded as positive.

VITRIOL. (1) Sulphuric acid. (2) Any sulfate of heavy metal.

VOIDANCE. (1) The act of vacating, emptying, voiding. (2) The state of being void; vacancy.

VOLATILE. (1) Changeable; easily influenced. (2) Evaporating rapidly at ordinary temperature upon exposure to air.

VOLT. (1) The unit of electromotive force or electric pressure analogous to water pressure in pounds per square inch. (2) Force if applied to a circuit having a resistance of one ohm will produce one ampere.

VOLTAGE. Difference in electrical potential; analogous to pressure.

VOLT AMPERE. The basic unit of apparent power. The *volt amperes* of an electric circuit are the mathematic product of volts and amperes.

VOLUME RATE. A special freight rate accorded shippers who agree to ship large quantities of certain commodities (e.g., a unit-train of coal).

VOLUTE. A spiral, scroll-like ornament at the top of a pillar; characteristic of an Ionic capital.

VOUCHER. An instrument of payment; a check or bank draft.

VOUSSOIRS. The individual stones forming an arch.

VOX POPULI. Voice of the people; public opinion.

VUG. An opening in a mining vein into which crystals may project.

VULCANIZE. To treat crude rubber with sulfur or sulfur compounds in varying proportions and different temperatures to increase its strength and elasticity.

W

WAGON-LIT (French). Sleeping car.

WAINSCOT. Lining of an interior wall with boards or paneling.

WAINWRIGHT. Repairer or maker of wagons.

WAIVE. (1) Abandon. (2) Forego. (3) Relinquish rights, claims, and/or privileges.

WALE. (1) One of a number of extra-thick planks on the side of a wooden vessel. (2) A strake.

WALING PIECE. A timber on the water side of a pier to prevent damage to the mainland structure by a vessel docking or at dockside.

WALKOUT. A workers' strike; a wildcat strike.

WALKUP. A building without elevators.

WALKWAY. A sidewalk, a passageway.

WALL PLATE. A horizontal timber for bearing the ends of joists, girders,

WALL PLUG. An electric outlet set in a wall.

WANIGAN. A place to store supplies in a logging camp.

WARD. (1) A person who is in the charge and protection of a guardian. (2) A political subdivision within a community.

WAREHOUSE. A structure for the storage of goods; an etape.

WAREROOM. A room in which goods are exhibited for sale.

WARRANT. (1) Sanction; authorize. (2) A short-term obligation issued by a governmental body in anticipation of revenue. (3) An instrument issued by a corporation giving the holder the right to subscribe to capital stock at a fixed price. (4) A paper issued by a court for the purpose of bringing a person into court; a document for arrest.

WARRANTEE. The person to whom a warrant is made or issued.

WARRANTER, WARRANTOR. One who gives or issues a warrant or warranty.

WARRANTY. A real covenant binding the grantor of an estate and his heirs to warrant and defend the title.

WARRANTY DEED. A deed guaranteeing good title free of liens and encumbrances and which will defend the grantee against all claims.

WASTAGE. Loss by use, decay, leakage, or through wastage or lack of attention.

WASTE. Material from an excavation or leveling process not of any use except as "fill."

WASTE BANKS. Banks outside a roadway formed by waste deposits.

WASTELAND. Barren and uncultivated land.

WATER BASIN. Watershed.

WATERCOURSE. Any stream of water.

WATER GAS. A poisonous mixture chiefly of hydrogen and carbon monoxide made by forcing steam over white-hot carbon, as coal or coke, and used for cooking, heating, or lighting.

WATERING PLACE. A health resort having mineral springs; a spa.

WATER MILL. A mill operated by water power.

WATER PARTING. (1) A summit or boundary line separating the districts of two streams or coasts. (2) A divide.

WATER RIGHT. A riparian right.

WATERSHED. (1) Water parting. (2) An area bounded by a water parting and draining ultimately to a particular body of water.

WATER SYSTEM. (1) A river with all its tributaries. (2) Water supply, including wells, purification facilities, pumping station, and main transportation system.

WATER TABLE. (1) A projecting ledge, as molding, running along the side of a building to shed precipitation. (2) The surface marking the upper level of a water-saturated area below ground.

WATERWORKS. The building and equipment to supply a water system.

WATT. (1) The electrical unit of power, or rate, of doing work. (2) The rate of energy transfer equal to one ampere flowing under a pressure of one volt as unity power factor. (Analogous to horsepower or foot pounds per minute—746 watts equals one horsepower.)

WAYBILL. A document prepared by a freight carrier containing details of a shipment, including description of the lading, route, and charges.

WAYS AND MEANS COMMITTEE. A legislative committee charged with devising methods and resources for raising required revenues for operations of a state, nation, or organization.

WAY STATION. An intermediate depot between principal stations or terminals of a railroad.

WEATHERBOARD. (1) Clapboard. (2) A board used for the outer covering, or veneer, of a wooden structure.

WEATHER STATION. A point at which meteorological readings and reports are made. (Located at many airports.)

WEATHER STRIP. A material for covering the joint of door or window to keep rain, snow, or air from entering a a building.

WEB. (1) A metal plate or sheet connecting heavy structural members. (2) Paper threaded through a printing press.

WEIR. A dam in a stream for the purpose of raising the water level or to divert its flow.

WELDMENT. A unit formed by welding together and assembling.

WELL CAR. A flat car with a depression or opening in the center to allow a load to extend below the normal floor level when it could not otherwise come within overhead clearance limits. Also called "well-hole car."

WELLHEAD. (1) Fountainhead. (2) The source of a spring or stream.

WESTERLY. (1) A *westerly wind* is one blowing *from* the west. (2) *Toward* the west is a directional indication.

WHALEBACK. A freight ship with a convex upper deck.

ships may lie alongside for loading and unloading; a dock; a pier.

WHARF. A structure built along the shore of navigable water so that ships may lie alongside for loading and unloading; a dock; a pier.

WHARFINGER. The operator of a commercial wharf.

WHATMAN. A drawing paper or board of high quality.

WHEELHOUSE. The pilot house of a vessel.

WHERRY. A light boat.

WHIFFLETREE. The pivotal swinging bar to which traces of a harness are fastened and by which the vehicle is drawn by a team of animals.

WHINSTONE. Any hard, dark-colored rock; traprock.

WHIPPLETREE. A whiffletree.

WHITE GAS. Lead-free gasoline.

WHITE HEAT. Heat hotter than red heat; about 1500° Centigrade.

WHITE LEAD. A heavy, poisonous, basic lead carbonate usually marketed as a paste or powder in linseed oil, having excellent covering capabilities and used chiefly in exterior paints.

WHITESMITH. A tinsmith.

WHITEWASH. A composition of lime and water used for whitening structural surfaces such as wooden fences.

WHITING. Calcium carbonate prepared as a fine powder used as a pigment and extender in putty, paper coating, etc.

WHOLE GALE. A wind having a speed force of 55 to 63 miles per hour.

WHOLLY-OWNED SUBSIDIARY. An affiliated company owned in its entirety by the parent company.

WHORL. The drum-shaped section of the lower part of a spindle.

WIDOW'S WALK. A railed observation platform atop a house.

WILDCAT. To prospect and drill experimental wells or mine shafts in a territory not known to be a producing area.

WILDCAT STRIKE. A strike affecting one plant of a local union and neither sanctioned not authorized by the national union.

WILDERNESS AREA. An area set aside by government for preservation of native and natural conditions.

WILDING. Not cultivated.

WILD LAND. Wasteland.

WIMBLE. (1) An auger. (2) Any instrument used for boring holes.

WINCH. (1) Any of various devices for hauling or pulling. (2) A machine with one or more drums on which to coil rope, cable, or hoisting. (3) A windlass.

WINDBREAK. Something, as a hedge or fence, that protects from, or breaks, the force of the winds.

WINDFALL. (1) A piece of unexpected good fortune. (2) A tract of land on which trees have been felled by the wind.

WINDFLAW. A sharp gust of wind.

WINDLASS. (1) Any of various devices for hauling or hoisting. (2) A horizontal barrel or axle supported on parallel vertical posts; when turned by crank or motor hoists, the rope or cable is wound around the barrel or axle. (3) A kind of winch.

WINDOW SASH. The framework in which panes of glass are set in a window.

WINDOWSILL. The horizontal member at the bottom of a window opening.

WINDWARD. Moving or situated toward the direction from which the wind is blowing.

WING AND WING. With sails extended on both sides of the boat.

WING LOADING. The gross weight of an airplane divided by the area of the wings.

WING WALL. An extension of an abutment wall to retain the adjacent earth.

WINZE. A steeply inclined passageway connecting a mine working place with a lower one.

WIREDRAW. To draw metal into a strand of wire.

WOLFRAMITE. A mineral consisting of iron manganese tungstate used as a source of tungsten.

WOODCOAL. (1) Charcoal. (2) Lignite.

WOOD PULP. Wood reduced to pulp and used in paper making.

WORK CAMP. (1) A prison camp. (2) A short-term group project participated in by volunteers. (3) A camp set up by construction workers working in remote areas.

WORKING CAPITAL. (1) The excess of current assets over current liabilities. (2) All capital of a business except that invested in capital assets.

WORKING DRAWING. A drawing made to scale for the direction of contractors and others.

WORK STOPPAGE. (1) Concerted cessation of work by a group of employes. (2) Cessation of operations of a plant brought about by a lack of raw materials or supplies.

WRAP AROUND MORTGAGE. An all-inclusive mortgage including all underlying financing after the down payment.

WRIT. A formal written statement or document.

WRIT OF EXECUTION. A writ which authorizes and directs the proper officers to carry into effect a decree of the court.

WRITE-DOWN. A deliberate reduction in the book value of an asset.

WRITE-OFF. (1) Depreciation. (2) To take off the books; cancel. (3) Reduce the estimated value or real value of something.

WROUGHT IRON. A commercial form of iron that is tough but malleable and relatively soft, containing less than 0.3 percent carbon and carrying one or two percent of slug mechanically mixed into it.

WYE TRACK. A triangular arrangement of railroad trackage by which locomotives, cars, and trains, may be rerouted in a direction opposite to which they had been headed.

X

XENOLITH. A fragment of rock included in another rock.
XERIC. Low or deficient in moisture for the support of life.

Y

YARD. A system of railroad tracks branching from a common lead track, with defined limits, used for switching, making up trains, or storing railroad cars.

YARDARM. Either end of the yard (cross spar) of a square-rigged vessel.

YARDMASTER. The person responsible for control of trains and engine operations within a railroad yard.

YARD MULE. A small tractor used to move semitrailers and other equipment around a terminal yard or factory storage area.

YAWL. A small boat rigged fore and aft and carrying a mainsail and one or more jibs with a mizzenmast far aft.

Z

ZEOLITE. Any of various hydrous silicates similar to feldspar.

ZINC WHITE. A white pigment, used especially in house paint and glazes, that consist of zinc oxide.

ZONING. A regulation which controls the use of property and places limitations upon the shape and size of buildings occupying the area. (Various zoning standards are included within these alphabetical listings, e.g., floating; non-conforming use; performance standards; special use; use; variance.)

ZONING BOARD. A zoning commission; a regulatory body ruling on zoning matters.

ZONING MAP. A land-use map indicating zoned areas.

ZONING ORDINANCE. Exercise of the police authority of a governmental subdivision in regulating the use of property through the enactment of zoning laws and regulations.

ZONING PLAN. A plan that divides the community into agricultural, residential, commercial, recreational, and industrial districts or zones. Special uses are sometimes included, such as public facilities, airports, etc.

The Handbook

Useful Information

ACREAGE, ESTIMATING. The simplest way to obtain the dimensions and acreage of a tract of land is to visit the courthouse of the county in which the property is situated and inspect the plat books and deed records to be found in the Recorder of Deeds' offices.

However, there may be times when that procedure is not feasible, i.e., the county seat is some distance from the property in question and you wish to have a general idea as to the acreage you are viewing at the moment.

While there are a number of ways of estimating the number of acres in a tract, certain rule of thumb dimensions are well to bear in mind. For example, a stride is about three feet. You should measure yours so that you will be prepared to more accurately pace off the boundaries of a property.

It is probable that a road will form at least one boundary so that you will be able to make a measurement from your car, bearing in mind that a tenth of a mile is equal to 528 feet.

The distance between telephone poles or local power line supporting poles is usually about 40 to 100, or more, feet. Step off the distance between two of these poles along the boundary of the tract, count the poles between the property lines, and this will provide a fairly accurate estimate of that boundary dimension.

A square acre is slightly less than 209 feet by 209 feet. (Actually, 208.711 feet by 208.711 feet.) Thus, it is relatively simple to estimate total acreage if one knows the extent of the boundaries of the property. Even in irregularly shaped pieces, reasonably accurate estimates may be made by "piecing together" the variously shaped tracts. First, "square off" the major portion of the property and ascertain the number of acres therein. Then piece together the remaining portions and add to the initial estimate.

It should be remembered that a "section" is a square mile containing 640 acres and that each "section line" is one mile from the next. Most rural county roads are spaced a mile apart, having generally been built along section lines. Hence, with that knowledge, fairly quick estimates may be made of acreage.

If one knows the number of square feet in a piece of land, acreage may be obtained by dividing the total number of square feet by 43,560 or by multiplying the total square footage by 23 and pointing off six decimal places from the right. (Example: $43,560 \times 23 = 1.001880$. The actual multiplier is 2295684.)

CONSTRUCTION AND MANUFACTURING OPERATIONS FACTS

1. Doubling the diameter of a pipe increases capacity four times.
2. Double-riveting is about 20 percent stronger than single.
3. For each square foot of grate surface, there are nine square feet of heating surface.
4. Thirty to forty pounds of water per hour are required for each boiler horsepower.
5. Steam boilers consume 12 pounds of coal for each square foot of grate surface.
6. Steam rising from water at its boiling point has a pressure equal to the atmosphere—14.7 pounds per square inch.
7. To find the pressure in pounds per square inch of a column of water, multiply the height of the column by .434.
8. One ton of coal is equivalent to two cords of wood for steam purposes.
9. One cubic foot of anthracite coal = 58 pounds; bituminous = 50 pounds.

COST OF LIVING INDEX (CONSUMER PRICE INDEX). The Consumer Price Index was initiated during World War I when rapid changes in living costs made such an index essential in wage negotiations. Studies of family expenditures were conducted in ninety-two industrial centers from 1917-1919. Over the years, people's buying habits have changed so that there have been various adjustments made in methods and scope of determining the base indices.

Today, the Consumer Price Index (CPI) is a statistical measure of changes in prices of goods and services bought by urban wage earners and clerical workers, including families and single persons. It measures changes in prices, which are the most important cause of changes in the *cost of living*, but does not indicate how much families actually spend for living expenses.

The Consumer Price Index is a weighted aggregative index number with "fixed" annual weights. It is often referred to as the Cost of Living Index, or "the market basket index."

The index represents changes in everything that people buy including: food; clothing; automobiles, parts and repairs; housing and home furnishings; fuel; drugs; recreational goods; transportation; restaurant meals; household utilities; etc. It deals with prices actually charged to consumers, including all taxes directly associated with the purchase of products and services, including sales and excise taxes.

Sampling for the index is taken in 56 selected cities by personal visits to a representative sample of nearly 18,000 stores. (Detailed information on this subject may be reviewed in the Bureau of Labor Statistics *Handbook of Methods,* Chapter 10.)

DEGREE-DAYS, HOW TO FIGURE.

For Heat Requirements: In order to figure a degree-day subtract the difference between the high and low temperatures of the day from 65° Fahrenheit, the "standard daily temperature" used in the United States. If, for example, the *low* was 32° and the *high* was 48° the difference would be 16°, which when subtracted from 65° indicates that for *that day* the degree-day was 49°. In the event that situation prevailed for a ten-day period (which would be unusual) the degree-days for that period would be 490 degree days.

To calculate required heating facilities, the BTU is used as a basis. Certain *loss factors* must be calculated, such as the type of building, insulation, window and door openings, prevailing winds, etc. Against those loss factors, there are certain *gain factors* such as the number of workers in the plant (generating X° body heat), the nature of the process (welding; heat treating, etc.)

It is obvious that heat engineers must be brought in to properly estimate the needs of any buildings with respect to heating and cooling.

For Cooling: Again, as above, the difference between high and low temperatures are determined and subtracted from 65°. And again, calculations must be made by experts to determine the required equipment for adequate cooling of the building.

ELECTRIC POWER. *The Index of Weekly Electric Output* is a weekly index of variations in the aggregate kilowatt hour output of the electric utility industry. It is representative of all energy contributing to the public supply and includes the output of both investor-owned and government-owned generating stations. *Frequency* refers to the number of cycles through which an alternating current passes per second. The U.S. standard is 60 cycles per second (60 hertz). *Heat Rate* is a measure of generating station thermal efficiency, usually expressed in BTU's per net kilowatt hour. It is computed by dividing the total BTU content of fuel burned for electric generation by the resulting net kilowatt generation.

Single-Phase Power is the ordinary service to households (120 v.). *Two-Phase Power* is a service required for appliances such as electric ovens, washer-dryers, and the like. *Three-Phase Power* usually is required by industry for the purpose of operating heavy machinery and equipment in a manufacturing plant.

LAND SITE IMPROVEMENT, ESTIMATED COSTS FOR.

Bore core test (four-inch) = $10 to $15 per foot.

Curb and gutter = $4.25 per linear foot.

Driveways and roadways (concrete)—25 ft. wide = $25 to $30 per linear foot; 40 ft. wide = $40 to $45 per linear foot.

Fire hydrants = $450 each.

Grading = 50¢ to $1.50 per cubic yard.

Percolation test = $60 per test hole.

Railroad sidetract or spur = $25 per linear foot (includes rails, ties, plates, spikes and ballast.)

Railroad switch (main line)—new = $10,000; related signal work = $15,000.

Sanitary sewer—8-inch = $9.50 to $12.50 per linear foot; 12-inch = $10 to $15 per linear foot; 18-inch = $14 to $19 per linear foot.

Sanitary sewer manholes = $650 to $700 each.

Sidewalks = $1 per square foot.

Site survey—40 acres = $18 to $25 per acre for five-foot contour boundary survey; 120 acres = $12 to $18 per acre for five-foot boundary survey.

Aerial Survey—40 acres = $15 to $18 per acre; 120 acres = $10 to $12 per acre.

Storm drain—12-inch = $9 to $13 per linear foot; 36-inch = $25 to $35 per linear foot; 60-inch = $65 to $75 per linear foot.

Storm drain manholes = $550 to $600 each.

Water lines—10-inch = $12 per linear foot; 12-inch = $14 per linear foot.

Water towers—200,000 gallon capacity = $125,000 minimum; 1,000,000 gallon capacity = $500,000 minimum.

Note: The above costs are based upon June 1973 costs. They should be used only as a guide, with adjustments made based upon local conditions.

SHIFT ANALYSIS AND INDUSTRIAL MIX. Even though employment in a community's industry may have increased in the current year over a base year, it may not have participated in economic growth as it should have. Here's how to find out:

Let us suppose that industry "A" (SIC 3301) has enjoyed an increase of fifty employees during the present year over the base year—a jump of 100 percent. Now let's see what has happened to total national employment: Suppose employment in all industries has increased by only 30 percent. This makes our local industry "A" look pretty good, doesn't it? However, further investigation indicates that total national "A" industries increased by 150 percent. This shows that our local industry "A" did better than the national economy as a whole, but failed to hold its own in its own industry classification at the national level.

Of course, employment increases aren't the only criteria upon which to make judgment. Sales, net income, and other elements should be considered before becoming pessimistic about local industry "A." It may be that new equipment may have stepped up productivity to the point that it was not neccessary to increase employment at the same rate as the nation as a whole.

Notwithstanding, local development organizations would do well to look into the matter of industrial "mix" of various companies in the community. It is conceivable that trouble may be brewing when the local industry appears to be falling behind others in the same business in the nation as a whole. There is a relatively easy formula to be followed in determining the standing of each industrial classification. Suppose we use local industry "A" mentioned above as the example. All figures used, of course, are fictitious:

	Base Year	This Year	% Inc.
(1) U.S. Total All Employment	60,000,000	80,000,000	30.0%
(2) U.S. Industry "A" Employment	100,000	250,000	150.0%
(3) Local Industry "A" Employment	5,000	10,000	100.0%

(Net increase—Local Industry "A"—5,000)

Natl. Growth—5,000 × 30.0%	=	1,500	=	Gain due to national growth in the total economy
Indu. Mix—5,000 × 120.0%				
(2)−(1)	=	6,000	=	Gain which should accrue to national growth in Industry "A."
Local Growth—5,000 × 50.0%				
(2)−(3)	=	−2,500	=	Loss at local level based on national growth in Industry "A."
Total	=	5,000*		

*This figure will always be the same as the Local Industry increase (or decrease) regardless of all other figures involved in the computation. If it is not, there is an error in the computations.

It should be remembered that there is no magic in the foregoing formulas or computations. Although the example given is directed toward a comparison of employment, similar method could be utilized for production per employee; net operating income, etc. The results are merely relative. They show the relationship of the local company's operations to total national growth (or loss) and to the industry classification at the national level.

Tables

BOND RATINGS

	Moody's			Standard & Poor's	
Rank	Rating	Quality Description	Rank	Rating	Description
1	Aaa	Best	1	AAA	Highest
2	Aa	High	2	AA	High
3	A	High Medium	3	A	Upper Medium
4	Baa	Lower Medium	4	BBB	Medium
5	Ba	Speculative Elements	5	BB	Lower Medium
6	B	Lack Characteristics of desirable Investment.	6	B	Speculative
7	Caa	Poor Standing	7	CCC	Outright Speculative.
8	Ca	Speculative —often in default.	8	CC	Outright Speculative.
9	C	Lowest	9	C	Income not paying interest.
			10	D	In default

COMPACTION PRESSURES

Bearing Material	Allowable Pressures* (Pounds per Square Foot)
Natural soil	3,000
Compact soil	2,000
Weathered limestone	4,000
Weathered claystone	3,000
Weathered sandstone	12,000
Weathered silty shale	10,000
Slightly weathered limestone	30,000
Slightly weathered claystone	8,000
Slightly weathered sandstone	30,000
Slightly weathered silty shale	16,000

*Maximum pressures permitted without need for reinforcement of substructure.

FRACTIONS,
THEIR DECIMAL EQUIVALENTS and ACREAGE in SQUARE FEET

Fractions	Decimal Equiv.	Acreage Sq. Ft.	Fractions	Decimal Equiv.	Acreage Sq. Ft.
⅛	.1250	5,445	2 ⅝	2.6250	114,345
¼	.2500	10,890	2 ¾	2.7500	119,790
⅜	.3750	16,335	2 ⅞	2.8750	125,235
½	.5000	21,780	3	3.0000	130,680
⅝	.6250	27,225	3 ⅛	3.1250	136,125
¾	.7500	32,670	3 ¼	3.2500	141,570
⅞	.8750	38,115	3 ⅜	3.3750	147,015
1	1.0000	43,560	3 ½	3.5000	152,460
1 ⅛	1.1250	49,005	3 ⅝	3.6250	157,905
1 ¼	1.2500	54,450	3 ¾	3.7500	163,350
1 ⅜	1.3750	59,895	3 ⅞	3.8750	168,795
1 ½	1.5000	65,340	4	4.0000	174,240
1 ⅝	1.6250	70,785	4 ⅛	4.1250	179,685
1 ¾	1.7500	76,230	4 ¼	4.2500	185,130
1 ⅞	1.8750	81,675	4 ⅜	4.3750	190,575
2	2.0000	87,120	4 ½	4.5000	196,020
2 ⅛	2.1250	92,565	4 ⅝	4.6250	201,465
2 ¼	2.2500	98,010	4 ¾	4.750	206,910
2 ⅜	2.3750	103,455	4 ⅞	4.8750	212,355
2 ½	2.5000	108,900	5	5.000	217,800

GEOGRAPHIC DIVISIONS OF THE U.S. BUREAU OF CENSUS,
REGIONAL GROUPING BY STATES

New England
Connecticut
Maine
Massachusetts
New Hampshire
Rhode Island
Vermont

Middle Atlantic
New Jersey
New York
Pennsylvania

East North Central
Illinois
Indiana
Michigan
Ohio
Wisconsin

West North Central
Iowa
Kansas
Minnesota
Missouri
Nebraska
North Dakota
South Dakota

West South Central
Arkansas
Louisiana
Oklahoma
Texas

South Atlantic
Delaware
District of Columbia
Florida

Georgia
Maryland
North Carolina
South Carolina
Virginia
West Virginia

East South Central
Alabama
Kentucky
Mississippi
Tennessee

Mountain
Arizona
Colorado
Idaho
Montana
Nevada

New Mexico
Utah
Wyoming

*Pacific**
Alaska
California
Hawaii
Oregon
Washington

*The Bureau of the Census will include Alaska and Hawaii in the Pacific Region. Some organizations, however, will, for the time being, report these two states as a separate region so as not to destroy the historic statistical series on the Pacific Region.

THE METRIC SYSTEM and U. S. EQUIVALENTS

LINEAR MEASUREMENTS

Unit	Number of Meters	Approximate U.S.
myriameter	10,000	6.2 miles
kilometer	1,000	0.62 mile
hectometer	100	109.36 yards
decameter	10	32.81 feet
meter	1	39.37 inches
decimeter	0.1	3.94 inches
centimeter	0.01	0.39 inch
millimeter	0.001	0.04 inch

AREA MEASUREMENTS

Unit	Number of Square Meters	Approximate U.S.
sq. kilometer	1,000,000	0.3861 sq. mi.
hectare	10,000	2.47 acres
are	100	119.60 sq. yards
centare	1	10.76 sq. feet
sq. centimeter	0.0001	0.155 sq. inch

VOLUME

Unit	Number of Cubic Meters	Approximate U.S.
decastere	10	13.10 cu. yards
13.10 cu. yards stere	1	1.31 cu. yards
decistere	0.10	3.53 cu. feet
cubic centimeter	0.000001	0.061 cu. inch

CAPACITY

Unit	Number of Liters	Approximate U.S.
decaliter	10	2.64 gallons
liter	1	1.057 quarts
1.057 quarts deciliter	0.10	0.21 pint
0.21 pint centiliter	0.01	0.338 fluidounce
milliliter	0.001	0.27 fluiddram

MASS AND WEIGHT

Unit	Number of Grams	Approximate U.S.
metric ton	1,000,000	1.1 tons
quintal	100,000	220.46 pounds
kilogram	1,000	2.2046 pounds
hectogram	100	3.527 ounces
decagram	10	0.353 ounce
gram	1	0.035 ounce
decigram	0.10	1.543 grains
centigram	0.01	0.154 grain
milligram	0.001	0.015 grain

METRIC SYSTEM IN THE UNITED STATES, CHRONOLOGY OF

1776—United States using the English inch-pound system.

1790—George Washington wants United States to set its own system of measurements. Thomas Jefferson chooses one using the decimal system. The Paris Academy of Science comes out with the metric system. For the next seven years, France is on and off the metric system and England stands pat with its inch-pound methods.

1821—John Quincy Adams thinks the metric system ideal but not in wide enough use for world trade standard.

1832—United States adopts the English inch-pound system.

1840—Metric system becomes the law in France.

1863—National Academy of Sciences recommends the metric system.

1866—Congressional committee reports bills to permit and encourage the metric system.

1875—United States and sixteen other nations sign treaty to set up the International Bureau of Weights and Measures.

1890—President Harrison receives the standards for U.S. meters and grams.

1896—Bill to make metric system legal dies.

1899—Metric system in use by forty nations in scientific areas

1916—American Metric Association founded.

1941-45—Difficulty experienced in two-system standards of allied weaponry and machinery.

1957—Russian Sputnik. U.S. regulation establishes metric system as basis of weaponry and related equipment.

1959—Secretary of Commerce announces need for new study.

1965—President of England's Board of Trade announces the United Kingdom's resolve to go metric in ten years.

1968—U.S. bill promoting a metric system study becomes law.

1972—U.S. Senate bill S2483 is approved by the Senate.

Mileage by Highway Between 48 State Capitals and D.C
("Rounded" mileages to the nearest "5")

	Albany	Annapolis	Atlanta	Augusta	Austin	Baton Rouge	Bismark	Boise	Boston	Cheyenne	Carson City	Charleston	Columbia	Columbus	Concord	Denver
Albany, NY	—	340	965	300	1815	1455	1635	2505	160	1755	2750	645	820	600	155	1800
Annapolis, Md	340	—	640	585	1540	1155	1595	2395	420	1645	2635	385	490	420	460	1655
Atlanta, Ga	965	640	—	1210	920	525	1515	2210	1045	1450	2405	485	220	550	1090	1410
Augusta, Maine	300	585	1210	—	2110	1725	1930	2800	165	2050	3045	920	1065	895	145	2095
Austin, Texas	1815	1540	920	2110	—	430	1345	1660	1945	1010	1710	1230	1135	1220	1970	920
Baton Rouge, La	1455	1155	525	1725	430	—	1530	2020	1560	1300	2080	935	745	935	1600	1210
Bismarck, ND	1635	1595	1515	1930	1345	1530	—	1035	1795	575	1410	1295	1615	1140	1785	675
Boise, Idaho	2505	2395	2205	2800	1660	2020	1035	—	1665	755	445	2140	2395	2000	2655	835
Boston, Mass	160	420	1045	165	1945	1560	1795	1665	—	1915	2910	755	900	745	70	1960
Carson City, Nev	2750	2635	2410	3045	1710	2080	1410	445	2910	995	—	2375	2625	2235	2900	1050
Charleston, W.Va	645	385	485	920	1230	935	1295	2140	755	1380	2375	—	385	170	795	1370
Cheyenne, Wyoming	1755	1645	1450	2050	1010	1300	575	755	1915	—	995	1380	1640	1240	1905	100
Columbia, SC	820	490	220	1065	1135	745	1615	2395	900	1640	2625	385	—	540	945	1600
Columbus, Ohio	600	420	550	895	1220	935	1140	2000	745	1240	2235	170	540	—	755	1235
Concord, NH	155	460	1090	145	1970	1600	1785	2655	70	1905	2900	795	945	755	—	1950
Denver, Colorado	1800	1655	1410	2095	920	1210	675	835	1960	100	1050	1370	1600	1235	1950	—
Des Moines, Iowa	1125	1010	890	1420	885	920	665	1390	1285	635	1630	770	1060	620	1275	680
Dover, Delaware	300	70	705	540	1610	1220	1590	2455	375	1705	2700	450	555	480	415	1715
Frankfort, Kentucky	800	615	410	1095	1020	735	1185	1970	945	1210	2205	205	450	200	950	1175

Harrisburg, Pa.	270	95	700	545	1570	1185	1475	2340	380	2585	375	1590	555	365	420	1600
Hartford, Conn.	95	325	955	260	1855	1465	1730	2600	100	2845	660	1850	810	650	140	1885
Helena, Montana	2225	2120	2050	2525	1705	1975	620	495	2390	885	1885	695	2210	1730	2380	785
Indianapolis, Ind.	765	590	505	1060	1055	805	1020	1840	920	2075	305	1080	600	170	915	1065
Jackson, Miss.	1315	1015	390	1585	530	160	1435	2005	1420	2070	785	1270	605	780	1465	1180
Jefferson City, Mo.	1125	955	675	1425	755	700	925	1545	1280	1780	650	790	875	535	1280	750
Lansing, Mich.	675	570	730	970	1300	1050	1035	1905	835	2150	400	1155	775	235	830	1200
Lincoln, Nebraska	1315	1200	1015	1610	800	960	600	1210	1475	1450	925	455	1205	790	1470	490
Little Rock, Ark.	1320	1045	505	1615	495	355	1175	1785	1450	1910	730	1035	725	725	1475	950
Madison, Wisconsin	945	590	820	1240	1165	995	695	1640	1105	1905	600	915	925	445	1095	960
Montgomery, Ala.	1135	810	170	1380	770	380	1545	2190	1220	2310	630	1430	375	660	1260	1375
Montpelier, Vermont	160	500	255	180	1950	1610	1770	2635	185	2380	800	1890	980	735	115	1935
Nashville, Tenn.	990	700	1125	1270	840	545	1260	1950	1105	2190	400	1195	445	395	1145	1155
Oklahoma City, Okla.	1500	1325	840	1795	400	600	955	1440	1655	1570	1020	695	1055	905	1655	605
Olympia, Washington	2875	2765	2700	3170	2200	2560	1250	540	3035	690	2535	1295	2855	2380	3030	1375
Phoenix, Arizona	2465	2290	1790	2760	985	1405	1465	970	2615	725	1985	890	2010	1870	2615	790
Pierre, SD	1565	1460	1380	1860	1140	1325	210	1080	1725	1375	1225	445	1545	1070	1720	525
Providence, RI	160	390	1015	205	1915	1525	1790	2660	45	2905	720	1910	870	715	110	1945
Raleigh, NC	615	285	370	860	1290	900	1620	2460	700	2700	1355	1705	205	495	730	1665
Richmond, Va.	460	130	505	705	1425	1035	1580	2445	545	2680	310	1690	360	450	585	1675
Sacramento, Calif.	2870	2760	2490	3165	1755	2165	1535	565	3030	135	2495	1115	2705	2360	3025	1175
St. Paul, Minn.	1195	1085	1075	1490	1140	1170	440	1445	1355	1765	855	805	1175	700	1350	850
Salem, Oregon	2935	2825	2655	3230	2110	2470	1310	450	3095	525	2590	1205	2845	2435	3085	1285
Salt Lake City, Utah	2205	2095	1900	2500	1295	1655	925	360	2365	545	1830	450	2090	1695	2355	510
Sante Fe, NM	1990	1820	1370	2290	685	1045	1030	975	2145	1090	1520	455	1590	1400	2145	355
Springfield, Ill.	935	780	605	1230	935	740	915	1655	1095	1890	500	900	770	365	1090	870
Tallahassee, Florida	1170	840	255	1415	885	460	1750	2395	1250	2495	705	1635	355	810	1290	1580
Topeka, Kansas	1305	1130	870	1600	680	810	745	1345	1460	1585	835	595	1060	710	1460	540
Trenton, NJ	195	155	780	430	1680	1290	1595	2465	270	2705	495	1710	635	490	310	1720
Washington, DC	355	30	610	600	1510	1120	1505	2375	435	2615	350	1625	465	395	480	1630

To approximate kilometers multiply mileage by 1.61.

Mileage by Highway Between 48 State Capitals and D.C. continued

	Nashville	Montpelier	Montgomery	Madison	Little Rock	Lincoln	Lansing	Jefferson City	Jackson	Indianapolis	Helena	Hartford	Harrisburg	Frankfort	Dover	Des Moines
Albany, NY	990	160	1135	945	1320	1315	675	1125	1315	765	2225	95	270	800	300	1125
Annapolis, Md.	700	500	810	590	1045	1200	570	955	1015	590	2120	325	95	615	70	1010
Atlanta, Ga.	255	1125	170	820	505	1015	730	675	390	505	2050	955	700	410	705	890
Augusta, Maine	1270	175	1380	1240	1615	1610	970	1425	1585	1060	2525	260	545	1095	540	1420
Austin, Texas	840	1950	770	1165	495	800	1300	755	530	1055	1705	1855	1570	1020	1610	890
Baton Rouge, La.	545	1610	380	995	355	960	1050	700	160	805	1975	1465	1185	735	1220	920
Bismarck, ND	1260	1770	1545	695	1175	600	1035	925	1435	1020	620	1730	1475	1185	1590	665
Boise, Idaho	1950	2635	2190	1640	1785	1210	1905	1545	2005	1840	495	2600	2340	1970	2455	1390
Boston, Mass.	1105	185	1220	1105	1450	1475	835	1280	1420	915	2390	100	380	945	375	1285
Carson City, Nev.	2190	2880	2310	1905	1910	1450	2150	1780	2070	2075	885	2845	2585	2205	2700	1630
Charleston, W.Va.	400	800	630	600	730	925	400	650	785	305	1885	660	375	205	450	770
Cheyenne, Wyoming . .	1195	1890	1430	915	1035	455	1155	790	1270	1080	695	1850	1590	1210	1705	635
Columbia, SC	445	980	375	925	725	1205	775	875	605	600	2210	810	555	450	555	1060
Columbus, Ohio	395	735	660	445	725	790	235	535	780	170	1730	650	365	200	480	620
Concord, NH	1145	115	1260	1095	1475	1470	830	1280	1465	915	2380	140	420	950	415	1275
Denver, Colorado	1155	1935	1375	960	950	490	1200	750	1180	1065	785	1885	1600	1175	1715	680
Des Moines, Iowa	635	1255	900	285	565	195	525	275	825	470	1160	1220	960	620	1075	—
Dover, Delaware	765	460	875	895	1110	1260	630	1015	1085	650	2180	280	120	645	—	1075
Frankfort, Kentucky . . .	240	930	505	490	575	775	365	445	625	165	1775	850	565	—	645	620

Harrisburg, Pa.	960	120	565	—	285	2065	535	1045	900	515	1145	1075	780	865	430	730
Hartford, Conn.	1220	280	850	285	—	2325	825	1330	1185	770	1415	1355	1040	1125	195	1010
Helena, Montana	1160	2180	1775	2065	2325	—	1610	1910	1400	1630	1060	1650	1290	2045	2360	1795
Indianapolis, Ind.	470	650	165	535	825	1610	—	645	365	245	625	555	325	570	900	290
Jackson, Miss.	825	1085	625	1045	1330	1910	645	—	550	890	865	260	835	240	1475	385
Jefferson City, Mo.	275	1015	445	900	1185	1400	365	550	—	575	355	350	435	665	1260	430
Lansing, Mich.	525	630	365	515	770	1630	245	890	575	—	715	805	345	805	810	525
Lincoln, Nebraska	195	1260	775	1145	1415	1060	625	865	355	715	—	605	715	1000	1450	760
Little Rock, Ark.	565	1110	575	1075	1355	1650	555	260	350	805	605	—	715	475	1455	345
Madison, Wisconsin	285	895	490	780	1040	1290	325	835	435	345	715	715	—	855	1075	565
Montgomery, Ala.	900	875	505	865	1125	2045	570	240	665	805	1000	475	855	—	1295	295
Montpelier, Vermont	1255	460	930	430	195	2360	900	1475	1260	810	1450	1455	1075	1295	—	1125
Nashville, Tenn.	635	765	240	730	1010	1795	290	385	430	525	760	345	565	295	1125	—
Oklahoma City, Okla.	550	1390	860	1275	1560	1375	735	575	425	975	410	340	825	795	1635	675
Olympia, Washington	1810	2830	2425	2715	2970	650	2260	2545	2050	2280	1710	2295	1935	2690	3010	2445
Phoenix, Arizona	1420	2350	1830	2235	2525	1130	1700	1400	1350	1910	1235	1320	1695	1645	2600	1655
Pierre, SD	490	1525	1110	1405	1665	695	950	1245	735	970	395	985	630	1380	1700	1125
Providence, RI	1280	340	910	345	70	2385	885	1390	1245	835	1475	1420	1100	1185	215	1070
Raleigh, NC	1095	350	505	370	605	2210	630	760	940	725	1250	870	925	545	775	525
Richmond, Va.	1060	195	515	215	450	2175	615	1365	960	625	1235	955	890	680	620	610
Sacremento, Calif.	1750	2820	2325	2705	2965	1010	2195	2150	1905	2275	1570	1995	2030	2390	3005	2310
St. Paul, Minn.	250	1150	745	1035	1290	1030	580	1050	510	600	395	815	255	1105	1330	820
Salem, Oregon	1840	2885	2420	2770	3030	705	2285	2455	1995	2335	1660	2235	1995	2640	3065	2400
Salt Lake City, Utah	1085	2155	1660	2040	2300	475	1530	1645	1240	1610	905	1440	1365	1870	2340	1645
Sante Fe, NM	945	1880	1350	1765	2050	1090	1230	1035	885	1435	755	875	1225	1275	2125	1210
Springfield, Ill.	290	845	330	730	1015	1450	190	585	200	375	445	455	260	635	1070	350
Tallahassee, Florida	1105	910	1280	905	1155	2250	760	425	870	985	1200	670	1055	205	1330	495
Topeka, Kansas	260	1195	630	1080	1365	1220	540	715	205	750	170	450	535	850	1440	615
Trenton, NJ	1080	105	685	120	175	2190	660	1155	1020	640	1270	1185	905	950	355	835
Washington, DC	990	100	545	110	345	2100	565	985	930	550	1180	1015	815	780	515	670

To approximate kilometers multiply mileage by 1.61.

Mileage by Highway Between 48 State Capitals and D.C. continued

	Oklahoma City	Olympia	Phoenix	Pierre	Providence	Raleigh	Richmond	Sacramento	St. Paul	Salem	Salt Lake City	Santa Fe	Springfield	Tallahassee	Topeka	Trenton	Washington, DC
Albany, NY	1500	2875	2465	1565	160	615	460	2870	1195	2935	2205	1990	935	1170	1305	195	355
Annapolis, Md.	1325	1765	2290	1460	390	285	130	2760	1085	2825	2095	1820	780	840	1130	155	30
Atlanta, Ga.	835	2700	1790	1380	1015	370	505	2490	1075	2655	1900	1370	605	255	870	780	610
Augusta, Maine	1795	3170	2760	1860	205	860	705	3165	1490	3230	2500	2290	1230	1415	1600	430	600
Austin, Texas	400	2200	985	1140	1915	1290	1425	1755	1140	2110	1295	685	935	885	680	1680	1510
Baton Rouge, La.	600	2560	1405	1325	1525	900	1035	2165	1170	2470	1655	1045	740	460	810	1280	1120
Bismarck, ND	955	1250	1465	210	1790	1620	1580	1535	440	1310	925	1030	915	1750	745	1595	1505
Boise, Idaho	1440	540	970	1080	2660	2460	2445	565	1445	450	360	975	1655	2395	2345	2465	2375
Boston, Mass.	1655	3035	2615	1725	45	700	545	3030	1355	3095	2365	2145	1095	1250	1460	270	435
Carson City, Nev.	1570	690	725	1375	2905	2700	2680	135	1765	525	545	1090	1890	2495	1585	2705	2615
Charleston, W.Va.	1020	2535	1985	1225	720	1355	310	2495	855	2590	1830	1520	500	705	835	495	350
Cheyenne, Wyoming	695	1295	890	445	1910	1705	1685	1115	805	1205	450	455	900	1635	595	1710	1625
Columbia, SC	1055	2855	2010	1545	870	205	360	2705	1175	2845	2090	1590	770	355	1060	635	465
Columbus, Ohio	905	2380	1870	1070	715	495	450	2360	700	2435	1695	1400	365	810	710	490	395
Concord, NH	1655	3030	2615	1720	110	740	585	3025	1350	3085	2355	2145	1090	1290	1460	310	480
Denver, Colorado	605	1375	790	525	1945	1665	1675	1175	850	1285	510	355	870	1580	540	1720	1630
Des Moines, Iowa	550	1810	1420	490	1280	1095	1060	1750	250	1840	1085	945	290	1105	260	1080	990
Dover, Delaware	1390	2830	2350	1525	340	350	195	2820	1150	2885	2155	1880	845	910	1195	105	100
Frankfort, Kentucky	860	2425	1830	1110	910	505	515	2325	745	2420	1660	1350	330	1280	630	685	545

	Oklahoma City, Okla.	Olympia, Washington	Phoenix, Arizona	Pierre, SD	Providence, RI	Raleigh, NC	Richmond, Va.	Sacramento, Calif.	St. Paul, Minn.	Salem, Oregon	Salt Lake City, Utah	Sante Fe, NM	Springfield, Ill.	Tallahassee, Florida	Topeka, Kansas	Trenton, NJ	Washington, DC
Harrisburg, Pa.	1275	2715	2235	1405	345	370	215	2705	1035	2770	2040	1765	730	905	1080	120	110
Hartford, Conn.	1560	2970	2525	1665	70	605	450	2965	1290	3030	2300	2050	1015	1155	2363	175	345
Helena, Montana	1375	650	1130	695	2385	2210	2175	1010	1030	705	475	1090	1450	2250	1220	2190	2100
Indianapolis, Ind.	735	2260	1700	950	885	630	615	2195	1050	2285	1530	1230	190	760	540	660	565
Jackson, Miss.	575	2545	1400	1245	1390	760	1365	2150	1050	1455	1645	1035	585	425	715	1155	985
Jefferson City, Mo.	425	2050	1350	735	1245	940	960	1905	510	1995	1240	885	200	870	205	1020	930
Lansing, Mich.	975	2280	1910	970	835	725	625	2275	600	2335	1610	1435	375	985	750	640	550
Lincoln, Nebraska	410	1710	1235	395	1475	1250	1235	1570	395	1660	905	755	445	1200	170	1270	1180
Little Rock, Ark.	340	2295	1320	985	1420	870	955	1995	815	2235	1440	875	455	670	450	1185	1015
Madison, Wisconsin	825	1935	1695	630	1100	925	890	2030	255	1995	1365	1225	260	1055	535	905	815
Montgomery, Ala.	795	2690	1645	1380	1185	545	680	2390	255	2640	1870	1275	656	205	850	950	780
Montpelier, Vermont	1635	3010	2600	1700	215	775	620	3005	1105	3065	2340	2125	1070	1330	1440	355	515
Nashville, Tenn.	675	2445	1655	1125	1070	525	610	2310	1330	2400	1645	1210	350	495	615	835	670
Oklahoma City, Okla.	—	1980	975	750	1620	1205	1285	1650	820	1890	1100	535	605	990	295	1395	1305
Olympia, Washington	1980	—	1380	1345	3035	2860	2820	695	800	165	900	1515	2100	2895	1865	2835	2745
Phoenix, Arizona	975	1380	—	1315	2585	2165	2265	770	1680	1230	650	495	1530	1830	1165	2360	2265
Pierre, SD	750	1345	1315	—	1725	1550	1510	1495	1620	1405	830	865	780	1585	555	1525	1440
Providence, RI	1620	3035	2585	1725	—	665	510	3030	400	3090	2365	2110	1075	1220	1425	235	405
Raleigh, NC	1205	2860	2165	1550	665	—	155	2820	1355	2910	2155	1735	825	560	1125	430	260
Richmond, Va.	1285	2820	2265	1510	510	155	—	2805	1180	2880	2140	1820	805	710	1145	275	105
Sacramento, Calif.	1650	695	770	1495	3030	2820	2805	—	1140	1885	535	665	1170	2575	1705	2830	2780
St. Paul, Minn.	800	1680	1620	400	1355	1180	1140	1885	—	535	1220	1140	480	1310	510	1155	1065
Salem, Oregon	1890	165	1230	1405	3090	2910	2880	535	1740	—	810	1425	2105	2845	1795	2895	2805
Salt Lake City, Utah	1100	900	650	830	2365	2155	2140	665	1220	810	—	610	1350	2070	1040	2165	2075
Sante Fe, NM	535	1515	495	865	2110	1735	1820	1170	1140	1425	610	—	1060	1460	685	1885	1795
Springfield, Ill.	605	2100	1530	780	1075	825	805	2015	480	2105	1350	1060	—	840	375	850	760
Tallahassee, Florida	990	2895	1830	1585	1220	560	710	2575	1310	2845	2070	1460	840	—	1050	985	815
Topeka, Kansas	295	1865	1165	555	1425	1125	1145	1705	510	1795	1040	685	375	1050	—	1200	1110
Trenton, NJ	1395	2835	2360	1515	235	430	275	2830	1155	2895	2165	1885	850	985	1200	—	170
Washington, DC	1305	2745	2265	1440	405	260	105	2740	1065	2805	2075	1795	760	815	1110	170	—

To approximate kilometers multiply mileage by 1.61.

MISCELLANEOUS MEASUREMENTS

LINEAR MEASUREMENTS

12 inches	= 1 foot
3 feet	= 1 yard; 36 inches
5½ yards; 16½ feet	= 1 rod; 1 pole; 1 perch
40 rods; 220 yards	= 1 furlong; ⅛ mile
8 furlongs	= 1 mile; 1760 yards; 5280 feet
3 miles	= 1 league

(Metric equivalents: 1 inch = 2.54 centimeters. 1 foot = 0.3048 meters. 1 yard = 0.9144 meters. 1 rod = 5.029 meters. 1 furlong = 201.17 meters. 1 mile = 1.6093 kilometers or 1609.3 meters.)

CHAIN MEASUREMENTS

7.92 inches	= 1 link
100 links or 66 feet	= 1 chain
10 chains	= 1 furlong; ⅛ mile
80 chains	= 1 mile

(Note: The engineer's chain is 100 feet long with links one foot long; thus 52.8 chains = 1 mile.)

SQUARE MEASUREMENTS

144 sq. inches	= 1 square foot
9 square feet	= 1 square yard
30 ¼ square yards	= 1 square rod
160 square rods	= 1 acre or 4840 sq. yds. or 43,560 sq. ft.

NAUTICAL MEASUREMENTS

6 feet	= 1 fathom
100 fathoms	= 1 cable's length. (There are variations of this, however. The British measure a cable's length at 608 feet; the U.S. Navy 720 feet or 120 fathoms.
1 sea mile (nautical)	= 1.1516 land miles
3 nautical miles	= 3.45 land miles
60 nautical miles	= 1 degree.

DRY MEASUREMENTS

1 pints	= 1 quart	=	67.20 cubic inches
8 quarts	= 1 peck	=	537.61 cubic inches
4 pecks	= 1 bushel	=	2150.42 cubic inches

U.S. government avoirdupois weights:

1 bushel of wheat	= 60 pounds
1 bushel of barley	= 48 pounds
1 bushel of oats	= 32 pounds
1 bushel of rye or corn	= 56 pounds
1 bushel of potatoes	= 60 pounds

LIQUID MEASUREMENTS

4 gills   = 1 pint   = 28.875 cubic inches
2 pints = 1 quart = 57.75 cubic inches
4 quarts = 1 gallon = 231 cu. in. = 8 pounds.

SURVEYOR'S MEASUREMENTS

625 square links   = 1 square pole
16 square poles   = 1 square chain
10 square chains = 1 acre
640 acres   = 1 square mile
36 square miles = 1 township

(Metric equivalents: 1 square mile = 259 hectares. 1 township = 9324 hectares or 93.24 sq. kilometers)

CUBIC MEASUREMENTS

1728 cubic inches = 1 cubic foot
27 cubic feet   = 1 cubic yard
16 cubic feet   = 1 cord foot (4×4×1)
128 cubic feet   = 1 cord (4×4×8)

(Metric equivalents: 1 cubic inch = 16.387 cubic centimeters. 1 cubic foot = 0.0283 cubic meter. 1 cubic yard = 0.7646 cubic meter. 1 cord = 3.625 cubic meters.)

CIRCULAR MEASUREMENTS

60 seconds = 1 minute
60 minutes = 1 degree
90 degrees = 1 quadrant
4 quadrants = 1 circle (360 degrees)

AVOIRDUPOIS WEIGHTS

16 drams   = 1 ounce
16 ounces = 1 pound or 7000 grains
14 pounds = 1 stone
100 pounds = 1 hundredweight
2000 pounds = 1 net ton; 1 short ton
2240 pounds = 1 gross ton; 1 long ton

TROY WEIGHTS (JEWELS)

3.086 grains   = 1 carat
24 grains   = 1 pennyweight
20 pennyweights = 1 ounce (Troy)
12 ounces   = 1 pound (Troy)

COMPARISON OF WEIGHTS

	Grain	Ounce	Pound
Avoirdupois	1	437½ gr.	7000 gr.
Troy	1	480 gr.	5760 gr.

175 pounds-Troy is equivalent to about 144 pounds-Avoirdupois

COMMODITY WEIGHTS AND MEASURES

One pint = One pound (water, sugar, berries, wheat, butter)
A gallon of milk weighs about 8.6 pounds; cream 8.4 pounds
A bale of cotton = 500 pounds
A bushel of coal = 80 pounds
A barrel of flour = 196 pounds
A barrel of meat or fish = 200 pounds
A barrel of cement = 4 bags = 376 pounds
A barrel of oil = 42 gallons
A keg of nails = 100 pounds.

NOISE LEVELS

EVERYDAY NOISES *(expressed in decibels)*

Ordinary conversation at one meter	60 dB
A whisper at one meter	30 dB
Private automobile	70 dB
Heavy motor truck	90 dB
Jet plane engine at 25 meters	140 dB
Busy street	80 dB

TYPICAL INDUSTRIAL PRODUCTION NOISE LEVELS IN A FACTORY*

Aircraft	105 dB
Apparel	90 dB
Chemicals	93 dB
Fabricated metal products	97 dB
Food processing, canning, etc	94 dB
Leather goods	96 dB
Lumber Products	99 dB
Machinery	99 dB
Paper, printing, publishing	96 dB
Primary metals	102 dB
Stone, clay and glass	94 dB
Textiles	92 dB

*Under the Occupational Safety and Health Act (OSHA) any industry with noise levels of 90 dB and above must provide a hearing conservation program for its employes.

TIME REQUIRED FOR A GIVEN PRINCIPAL TO DOUBLE ITSELF

Rate of Interest	Years at Simple Interest	Years at Compound Interest	
		Compounded Annually	Compounded Semi-Annually
4.5	22.23	15.748	15.576
5.0	20.00	14.207	14.036
6.0	16.67	11.896	11.725
7.0	14.29	10.245	10.075
8.0	12.50	9.006	8.837
9.0	11.11	8,043	7.874
10.0	10.00	7.273	7.000+

VOLUME FORMULAS

Figure	Formula	Explanation
cube	$V=a^3$	a=one of the dimensions
rectangular prism	$V=ABC$	A=length; B=width; C= depth
pyramid	$V=\dfrac{Ah}{3}$	A=area of base; h=height
cylinder	$V=\text{pi }r^2h$	pi=3.1416; r=radius; h=height
cone	$V=\dfrac{\text{pi }r^2h}{3}$	see cylinder
sphere	$V=\dfrac{4\text{ pi }r^3}{3}$	pi=3.1416; r=radius

WATER FACTS

The following is a list of minerals usually found in water and their effect on industrial equipment and products.

Minerals	Effect
Bicarbonate	Taste
Calcium	Will form insoluble curds in pipes and boiler tubes.
Chloride	Taste and increases corrosiveness.
Fluoride	May mottle enamelware.
Iron	In excess of 0.25 part per million will stain cloth, porcelain, and some other materials. Adds to water hardness.
Magnesium	Will form insoluble curds in pipes and boiler tubes.
Manganese	In excess of 0.25 parts per million will stain cloth, porcelain, and some other materials.
Nitrate	Large amounts of nitrate indicates pollution.
Potassium	Will cause foaming in boilers under certain conditions, especially in large amounts.
Silica	Causes boiler scale.
Sulfate	Can form permanent hardness and scale.

HARD WATER

Hard water can cause considerable corrosion and scale necessitating replacement of boilers and equipment. Relative hardness may be indicated as follows:

Hardness	Classification
Less than 15 ppm	Very soft water
15 to 50 ppm	Soft
50 to 100 ppm	Medium hard
100 to 200 ppm	Hard
Over 200 ppm	Very hard

WATER DEMAND (Selected Industries)

Typical water requirements for various types of industries:

Industry	Number of Gallons Required
To produce:	
One ton of bromine	5,000,000
One ton of synthetic rubber	600,000
One ton of aluminum	320,000
One ton of steel	65,000
One ton of coke from coal	3,600
One ton barrel of beer	470
One barrel of petroleum	770

WIND CHILL TABLE

When the Thermometer Reads:	When the wind at the miles per hour indicated below, it reduces temperature to:							
	Calm	5	10	15	20	25	30	35	40
+50	50	48	40	36	32	30	28	27	26
+40	40	37	28	22	18	16	13	11	10
+30	30	27	16	9	4	0	−2	−4	−6
+20	20	16	4	−5	−10	−15	−18	−20	−21
+10	10	6	−9		−25	−29	−33	−35	−37
0	0	−5	−21	−36	−39	−44	−48	−49	−53
−10	−10	−15	−33	−45	−53	−59	−63	−67	−69
−20	−20	−26	−46	−58	−67	−74	−79	−82	−85
−30	−30	−36	−58	−72	−82	−88	−94	−98	−100
−40	−40	−47	−70	−88	−96	−104	−109	−113	−116
−60	−60	−68	−95	−112	−124	−133	−140	−145	−148

WIND FACTS

BEAUFORT SCALE

Beaufort Number	Name	Miles per Hour	Description
0	Calm	Less than 1	Calm; smoke rises vertically.
1	Light Air	1-3	Direction of wind shown by smoke.
2	Light breeze	4-7	Wind felt on face; leaves rustle.
3	Gentle breeze	8-12	Leaves and small twigs in motion; wind extends a light flag.
4	Moderate breeze	13-18	Raises dust and loose paper.
5	Fresh breeze	19-24	Small leaved trees begin to sway; crested wavelets form on inland waters.
6	Strong breeze	25-31	Large branches in motion; telegraph wires whistle.
7	Moderate gale	32-38	Whole trees in motion walking difficult.
8	Fresh gale	39-46	Breaks twigs off trees.
9	Strong gale	47-54	Slight structural damage occurs.
10	Whole gale	55-63	Trees uprooted; considerable damage.
11	Whole gale	64-75	Widespread damage.
12	Hurricane	Above 75	Devastation.

Sample Forms

BUILDING LISTINGS

\# _____

LOCATION: (City) _____ (County) _____ (State) _____

SIZE: (Total Square Footage) _____ LAND AREA: _____

GENERAL DESCRIPTION:

    Number of Floors _____ Age _____ Condition _____

    Office Area s.f. _____ Parking (No. cars) _____

    Former use _____

DIMENSIONS:

    Length _____ Width _____ Column Spacing _____ × _____

    Ceiling Height (Eaves) _____ (Under Truss) _____

    Floor Load _____ Thickness _____

TYPE OF CONSTRUCTION: _____

UTILITIES IN BUILDING:

    Electric power _____

    Gas _____

    Water _____

    Sewer _____

    Boiler(s), Capacity and Condition _____

PROTECTIVE SERVICES:

    Sprinklers? _____ Security? Fenced? _____

    Local Fire Rating _____ Police Protection _____

OWNERSHIP: _____

AVAILABILITY AND PRICE: _____

This Listing Prepared by _____

        Date _____

INDUSTRIAL PROSPECT QUESTIONNAIRE (Suggested)

Name of
Company _____ Principal Products _____

Name of Company Contact _____ Title _____

Address _____

May company name be used? Yes ☐ No ☐
May other contact? Yes ☐ No ☐

A. LOCATION:

    1. Area of primary interest _____

    2. Size of community desired (Max. Pop.) _____ (Min. Pop.) _____

    3. Primary markets _____

    4. Raw materials and present source _____

B. TRANSPORTATION (Check)

    1. Freight: a. Truck ☐ b. Rail ☐ c. Air ☐ d. Water ☐ Local only ☐

    2. Passenger: a. Bus ☐ b. Rail ☐ c. Air ☐ d. Executive Plane ☐

    3. Workers: a. Public Bus ☐ b. Company Bus ☐ c. Private Cars ☐

C. EMPLOYMENT

    1. Immediate: a. Male _____ b. Female _____   (List required skills on reverse side of the form together with housing needs for key employees.)
    2. Ultimate: a. Male _____ b. Female _____

D. SITE REQUIREMENTS

    1. Acreage Required _____ 2. Dimensions _____ × _____

    2. Is industrial park location of particular interest? _____

E. BUILDING REQUIREMENTS

    1. Existing _____ New _____ 2. Sq. Ft. _____

    3. No. Floors _____ 4. Floor Load _____

    5. Min. Ceiling Ht. _____ 6. Minimum Column Spacing _____ ×

    _____

7. Sprinklers? _____ Air Conditioning? _____ Other? _____

No. Truck Doors _____ No. Railroad Doors _____ 9. Craneways _____

F. UTILITIES REQUIRED

   1. Electricity: (KW Load) _____ (KWH/Mo.) _____ (Peak Load) _____

   2. Gas: (Process—Cu. Ft./Mo.) _____ (Heat—Cu. Ft./Mo.) _____

   3. Water: (Process—Gal./Day) _____ (Sanitary—Gal./Day) _____

   4. Sewage: (Gal./Day) _____ (Type) _____

G. SKILLS REQUIRED

Number Male   Number Female

_____

_____

_____

_____

_____

_____

H. HOUSING REQUIREMENTS

   1. Number of executive units needed _____ Price range _____

   2. Number of supervisory units needed _____ Price range _____

   3. Other _____

I. FINANCIAL REQUIREMENTS

   1. Land Site _____

   2. Building _____

   3. Equipment _____

   4. Working Capital _____

(In each case indicate the amount required and the extent of local-state-federal financing desired. Indicate also if you have had other facilities so financed.)

J. REMARKS

_____

_____

_____

Information compiled by   (NAME AND TITLE)

    Date _____

LAND LISTINGS *(Suggested Form)*

L— _____

LOCATION: (City) _____ (County) _____ (State) _____

ACREAGE: _____ Inside City Limits _____ Outside _____

BOUNDARIES: North _____ ft.

                 East_____

                 South _____

                 West _____

TOPOGRAPHY: _____

ZONING: _____

PRESENT USE: _____

UTILITIES: Water _____

          Sewer _____

          Electricity _____

          Gas _____

TRANSPORTATION: R.R. _____

                     Highway _____

                     Air _____

OWNERSHIP: _____

AVAILABILITY AND PRICE: _____

SOURCE OF THE DATA: _____

This listing prepared by _____

               Date _____

OPTION TO PURCHASE REAL ESTATE

THIS AGREEMENT made and executed this _____ day of
_____, 19____, between _____ (NAME AND ADDRESS
parties of the first part, and _____ (NAME AND ADDRESS) _____ ,
parties of the second part: WITNESSETH that the parties of the first part,
themselves, their heirs, administrators or assigns, in consideration of the
sum of _____ ($) _____ paid by them to the parties of the second part and
accepted by the parties of the second part and acknowledged by them that
said payment represents the exclusive right (or option) to purchase at any
time within _____ (TIME FRAME) _____ from the date hereof, all the certain
_____ (PROPERTY) _____ located at _____ as more fully described in the following:

_____

_____

_____

for the total consideration of _____ ($) _____ to be payable in the following
manner:

_____

Witness(es):   Principals

_____

_____

_____

(May also be sworn to before Notary Public.)

PROSPECTING FOR INDUSTRY (Developer's Check List)

PART I—WHO THEY ARE

A. *Local*

1. Expansion of existing companies
2. Development of new enterprises
   a. Inventions and new products
   b. Locally-financed youth enterprises
   c. Local suppliers to existing companies.

B. *State*

1. Relocation within the state
2. Branch (expansion) within the state
   a. Good geographical location
   b. Need for additional labor
   c. Supplier for new company
   d. Desire expansion outside present location

C. *National*

1. Relocation (Cannot receive any federal assistance)
   a. Labor problems—wage rates; availability; etc.
   b. Customer migration out of present area of operations
   c. New customer development—new markets
   d. Financial inducements—tax relief, etc.
2. Expansion (branch plant)
   a. New market area
   b. Desire to split into smaller manufacturing plants
   c. New products
   d. New raw material and/or supply source

D. *International*

1. Overseas. Many companies are locating plants in foreign companies. However, opportunities of developing export-import trade for local, existing companies may be at hand.
2. Foreign companies
   a. Actual new plant location in the United States
   b. Purchase of interest in American firms
3. Relocation within the United States of American firms to take advantage of export-import rates and service

PART II—HOW AND WHERE TO FIND THEM

A. *Local*

    1. Frequent, regular calls on local businesses to offer services and assistance and discuss:
        a. Problems
        b. Projects
        c. Plans

    2. Meetings.
        a. Trade Associations; Chambers of Commerce
        b. Service Clubs
        c. Church Affairs
        d. Civic Events
        e. Social Events
        f. Political Gatherings

    3. Out-of-town visitors

B. *State*

    1. State Development Agency (e.g., Department of Commerce)
    2. State Chamber of Commerce
    3. State Manufacturers' Association
    4. Labor Organizations
    5. Utilities and Transportation Companies
    6. Engineering and Consulting Firms
    7. Governmental Bodies
    8. Participation in Seminars, etc.
    9. Personal calls on industries within the state
    10. Advertising, brochures, factual data
    11. State newspapers

C. *National and International*

    1. Federal agencies such as U.S. Dept. of Commerce
    2. Congressional representatives
    3. Financial journals and Trade publications
    4. Visitiations to centers of trade and business such as Chicago, New York, San Francisco, etc.

SELECTED LIST OF PROFESSIONAL ORGANIZATIONS

American Industrial Development Council (AIDC)
Suite 707
215 West Pershing Road
Kansas City, Missouri 64108

AIDC Educational Foundation
P.O. Box 495
Wenham, Massachusetts 01984

American Institute of Planners (AIP)
917 15th Street, NW
Washington, D.C. 20005

Associated General Contractors of America
1957 E Street, NW
Washington, D.C. 20006

Association of American Railroads
1920 L Street, NW
Washington, D.C. 20036

Edison Electric Institute
1015 18th Street
Washington, D.C. 20036

National Assn. of Industrial Parks
1601 North Kent Street
Arlington, Virginia 22209

National Assn. of Real Estate Boards
925 15th Street, NW
Washington, D.C. 20005

National Assn. of State Development Agencies
2000 K Street, NW
Washington, D.C. 20006

Society of Industrial Realtors
925 15th Street, NW
Washington, D.C. 20005

Urban Land Institute
1200 18th Street, NW
Washington, D.C. 20036

BIBLIOGRAPHY

Definitions: The Railway, Samuel Seeman. Published by the Penn Central Transportation Co. Philadelphia, Pa. 1971. Free

Glossary of Electric Utility Terms, Prepared by the Statistical Committee of the Edison Electric Institute. Published by the Electric Energy Association 90 Park Avenue, New York, N.Y. 10016 Publication #70-40 1970. $1.00

Guide to Industrial Development, Richard (Dick) Howard. Published by Prentice-Hall. $29.95

Industrial Real Estate, William N. Kinnard, Jr. and Stephen D. Messner. Published by Society of Industrial Realtors, 925 15th St., N.W., Washington, D.C. 20005. First Edition 1967; revised 1971; currently being again revised. $12.50

Practice of Industrial Development, Howard D. Bessire. Published by Hill Publishing Col, El Paso, Texas. $10.00

Questions and Answers on Real Estate, Robert W. Semenow. Published by Prentice-Hall. First Edition 1960; 7th Edition, 1972. $9.95

Techniques of Industrial Development, Howard D. Bessire. Published by Hill Publishing Co., El Paso, Texas. $10.00

Truck Drivers Dictionary and Glossary, Jean M. Walker. Published by American Trucking Associations, 1616 P St., N.W. Washington, D.C. 20036. 1972. Free

Universe of Industrial Development, Richard Preston. Published by the American Industrial Development Council Educational Foundation, Wenham, Mass. 01984. First Edition 1968; Revised 1971. $3.50

(Note: a new comprehensive work, *Industrial Development*, is to be published by Lexington Books in early 1975. Dr. Henry Hunker, the author, is Professor of Economic Geography at Ohio State University and is a nationally recognized authority in the field.)

About the Author

Koder M. Collison is a Fellow of the American Industrial Development Council and a Certified Industrial Developer. His experience in economic development spans more than three decades and includes administration of development programs at the local, state, regional, and national levels. In 1959, Governor Michael DiSalle appointed him to be the first director of Ohio's Department of Industrial and Economic Development Department (now the Department of Economic and Community Development). Later, Mr. Collison was named Commissioner of the West Virginia State Department of Commerce. Since 1965, he has been Director of Industrial Development for the Appalachian Regional Commission.